20P

JOSEPHINE

Josephine

by *MARIA GRIPE*

WITH DRAWINGS BY

Harald Gripe

translated from the Swedish by
Paul Britten Austin

CHATTO & WINDUS
LONDON

Published by
Chatto & Windus Ltd
40–42 William IV Street
London W.C.2.

ISBN 0 7011 0296 9

Text © 1961 Maria Gripe
Illustrations © 1961 Harald Gripe
Translation © 1970 Dell Publishing Co., Inc.

Originally published in Sweden under the title
Josefin by Albert Bonniers Forlag, Stockholm.
First published in this edition 1971
Second impression 1975

Printed and bound in Great Britain by
Redwood Burn Limited
Trowbridge & Esher

JOSEPHINE

I

ACTUALLY, her name isn't Josephine, and it isn't Joandersson, either.

Her name is Anna Grå.

It's rather a lovely name, if it happens to suit you. But she feels too small for it. To be called Ann Gray —because that's what the name means in Swedish —is rather like wearing shoes that are too big. You keep walking right out of them. So you have to put them away in the cupboard until they fit.

You can do that with names, too, if they won't keep step. At least that's what she's done.

She taught herself to write Anna Grå. Then she wrote it on the bottom of a cardboard box in capital letters, put the lid on, and hid it away at the back of her cupboard.

So, there's Anna Grå, waiting for her to grow up enough to *be* Anna Grå.

Meanwhile, she has to have another name. That shouldn't be hard. There are heaps to choose from.

Her first name must be as unusual as possible. Lots of people can share her last name.

Absolutely no one in the village is called *Josephine*. But most of them are called Johansson or Andersson. If you put these two together, you get Joandersson, so that twice as many people share that name.

Josephine Joandersson is a nice jolly name, a name to make anyone happy.

Josephine is one person and no one else: Joandersson means thousands and thousands of people.

And that's just as it should be!

She wants to be called Josephine Joandersson.

So much for Anna Grå. She's been forgotten.

Mandy cooks the meals at the vicarage, where Josephine lives. She's an important person. Sometimes, as she stirs the contents of her steaming saucepans or kneads her dough, she has the strangest things to tell, mostly about the World and Man.

Sometimes she talks about how big the world is, and how small people are. And she describes man's littleness on our huge earth in long words.

Josephine listens to her every time with the same awe and delight.

It's not easy to understand what Mandy means.
After all, anyone can see that Mandy isn't particularly small. In fact, she's the biggest person at the
vicarage. Mandy's arms and hands are the largest
Josephine has ever seen. And yet Mandy assures her
that on this earth she's only a tiny midge, a defenceless little insect, a dot.

Josephine can't take her eyes off Mandy. She's
round like a dot, that's true; but she certainly isn't a
small dot. And Josephine can't imagine anyone less
defenceless than Mandy.

Her voice isn't like an insect, either—that's a fact.

[3]

No voice in the vicarage makes itself heard more loudly.

Yes, Mandy is certainly full of riddles!

At other times she sighs and says that the world is getting smaller and smaller. This often happens as she flips through the newspapers.

"Is it shrinking, then?" asks Josephine.

"Yes, indeed," says Mandy. "It's shrinking a bit every day."

"Like my blue jumper in the wash?"

"Exactly."

That sounds terrible. Josephine's jumper has got so small, she can't wear it any more. Is this what's going to happen to the whole world?

"Can we grow out of it, Mandy?" asks Josephine.

"Out of what?"

"The world. Is it getting too small for us?"

"Yes," says Mandy. "You're getting to be as wise as a prophet, Miss Josephine."

Mandy loses herself in the newspaper. But now Josephine is really worried.

"What'll we do, then?" she asks, pulling the paper away from Mandy. "If there isn't enough room for us?"

Mandy's spectacles slide down to the tip of her nose. She gives Josephine a reassuring look.

"No danger of that," she says. "Because, you see, Josephine, we're getting smaller too."

Wide-eyed, Josephine stares at Mandy's huge bulk.

"Are you shrinking, too, Mandy?"

"Of course. You see, Miss Josephine, the world is just a tiny star among all the other little stars in the sky. And all of us are only little specks of dust. One fine day we may fly off to the moon, who knows . . ."

So Mandy and Josephine chat in the kitchen of the vicarage; and to Josephine it becomes clearer and clearer that it's a very strange world she's living in.

It's hard to be sure of anything.

For example, everyone says the world is as round as a ball—while anyone can see for himself that it's flat.

But, big or little, flat or round, one thing is sure: it's *old*.

The church is old, too: so old, no one knows who built it.

"And it's no use worrying about that," says Mandy. "Old churches like these, no one builds them. They just grow up by themselves. Look at the roof! Doesn't it look as if it'd grown straight up out of the earth?"

Yes, it really does.

The church is just across the road. Beside it stands a wooden bell tower with two bells that ring out ponderously, making the air quiver and roll in waves. It has been ringing like that for hundreds and hundreds of years. And when the sky is blue, the sound goes straight up, flying like a swallow. But when the sky is grey, then the sound becomes heavy and groans, like thunder over the forest.

Josephine isn't scared of the church bells. She is used to them. She has heard them ever since she was born.

Behind the church lies a field. There are bells there, too, but they're tiny little flowers and ring so quietly you can hardly hear them—though Josephine says she has. The field is called Bell Meadow. And there everything is new: the flowers and the grass are new each year.

Otherwise everything is as old as can be. The linden trees in the avenue and the oak in the paddock. The oak is terribly old and has a hole in it.

And the vicarage is old, too, of course . . .

The bed she sleeps in, the chair she's sitting on, the

sofa and the chest-of-drawers in Josephine's room, all of them are old.

And Mandy. Isn't she sometimes called *Old* Mandy?

Josephine has six brothers and sisters. But they're grown up and don't live at the vicarage any more, except Agneta, who is going to be married soon.

If one didn't know they were her brothers and sisters, one would take them for ordinary uncles and aunts, Josephine thinks, they are so big. Josephine herself is six, seven this winter.

She is quite small for her age: no one believes she is going to start school this autumn. But she is!

She has to start school; after all, she is an aunt! And was, even *before* she was born!

How would it look if a couple of her nephews were going to school—and not she, their aunt?

Papa-Father is the church's vicar.

He has lived for many years, Josephine knows. She doesn't know exactly *how* many; not a hundred, certainly, but far more than she can count. That doesn't matter, though, because his years don't make him old.

Sometimes he pretends to be old, particularly with Josephine. Like the time when he came and wanted her to call him Father, instead of Papa.

"You are so little, and have such an old Papa," he said, and made himself seem old and serious.

Josephine just laughed, but he was stubborn. She *must* say Father, he said. He looked tall and slim: his face moved about high above Josephine's. When she said Father, it was as if his face rose slowly to an even greater height, so that she could never reach it again.

Then she hit on the idea of calling him Papa-Father, and he agreed.

To say Papa-Father is like holding a balloon. Papa is the string and Father the balloon. If she weren't allowed to say Papa before Father, it would feel as if she had let go of the string and let the balloon fly straight up into the sky.

This would be particularly dangerous with Papa-Father, who is a clergyman and thinks a lot about heaven.

Mostly he is not to be disturbed. The two big brown doors to his room are almost always closed. And no one is allowed to open them. Anyway, she can't. The door handles are big and heavy; you can hang your whole weight on them and still they won't open. Though that's something she doesn't do any more—only when she was little.

But the doors remind her of Papa-Father. It makes you feel safe just to stand there, knowing he's inside.

There he sits, writing his sermon. "Sermon" is what his Big Talk in church on Sunday is called. He talks all by himself, and no one is allowed to interrupt—no one, because he's talking about Old Man God.

Everyone knows who Old Man God is. He's the oldest person on earth and in heaven. He's older than anything else that exists, because he was there first and made everything, all by himself. In his pictures, too, he looks old and tired. Josephine has a picture of him, in a book she was given by Papa-Father. He's a fine old fellow with white hair and a beard. Josephine calls him Old Man God.

But Old Man God's son—you can't help feeling sorry for him. He grew so quickly, he was almost never small—just a baby for a little while. But then, suddenly, he grew up and got into all sorts of trouble. He never had time to play, it all went so quickly. In the end he flew up to heaven—just like a balloon without a string.

Sometimes Josephine wonders about her own brothers and sisters. Did growing up happen to them just as quickly? Poor things—maybe they never had time to play either?

And what will happen to her? She wants to go on playing and playing . . .

2

"YOU NEVER THINK about anyone except yourself," sobs Agneta, and throws Josephine out. "I don't want to see you. You're mean! Go away!"

The door slams, and behind it Agneta bursts into tears.

Her feelings deeply hurt, Josephine goes downstairs.

Grown-ups are silly. And Agneta is the silliest of all. But there was a time, not so terribly long ago, when Agneta used to be nice and kind. That was before she met Eric, whom she's going to marry. In those days she always had time for Josephine. That Eric fellow spoiled everything.

Agneta would never have made a fuss about such

a little thing before. She would have just laughed.
Why should she cry and carry on so, just because
Josephine clipped a few butterflies out of her wedding veil? How was she to know it was a wedding
veil—with all those bits of cloth lying about Agneta's
room? The rest of them were clipping and snipping
all day long. Mama and Agneta and Miss Blom, the
seamstress! And they cut out huge pieces! All she'd
cut out were seven little ones. Anyone could tell you
how little stuff is needed for a small butterfly. Or
even for seven.

And yet Agneta begrudged it. Why, you can
hardly see the seven tiny holes in her veil, there's
such a lot of cloth in it. She'd never have thought
Agneta was so stingy.

And then . . . to say that Josephine only thinks
of herself!

That's really unfair. Josephine, who had been
meaning to give everyone in the house a butterfly!
Even Eric, though she doesn't really like him. That's
why she took seven. One in reserve, in case one went
wrong. It isn't all that easy, believe me, to sew seven
butterflies.

But she wouldn't dream of giving them any. Josephine is going to forget them—the whole bunch of
them.

Grown-ups are childish and mean. They have all
taken Agneta's side. Now they're sitting in there

with her, consoling her, coddling her as if she were a baby. Mama and Mandy and Miss Blom. But Agneta just keeps on snivelling. To make them sorry for her, of course.

No one bothers about Josephine. Forgotten, thrown out—that's her lot. All because of seven little butterflies. No one is ever sorry for her, just because she's not so quick to start snivelling as *some people*!

Well, they won't have to see her ever again. They'll regret it. She's going to disappear.

Yes, disappear . . .

It is still morning, a lovely morning in May. Spring is bursting forth.

The air is full of sounds. The buzz of bumble-bees and the twitter of birds. Resounding smacks of carpets being beaten. Down in the village people are laughing and calling out to each other. A boy whistles, a girl is singing, a milk cart creaks and rattles its empty bottles.

Everyone seems happy. Which only makes Josephine's grief heavier to bear.

There she walks, all by herself, along the dusty country road—away from the vicarage for ever.

In one hand she carries a little bag with three brushes in it: one for her teeth, one for her hair, and one for her shoes. These make up her toilet things. After all, one has to keep oneself clean and tidy, even if one has run away. One's shoes get so terribly dusty from walking all the time. Her hair is so fine, Mama says it has to be brushed morning and evening. Angel-fluff, Papa-Father calls it. At this thought Josephine gives a violent sniff: well, that's the last he'll ever see of angel-fluff.

In her bag she also carries a couple of pieces of toast, half a tube of caviar, the kind you get from the grocer's, three boiled potatoes, and a slice of cold pancake.

A very shabby and sad-looking monkey is also leaving with her. Josephine let him come because he's just as miserable as she is. On a terrible day like this a happy, well-stuffed teddy bear would have been out of place.

Josephine walks past the school where she was to have started classes this autumn. Now she can't. She looks at it a long time, pausing a moment at its gate.

"Good-bye school," she lisps in a melancholy voice. "Good-bye, Teacher, and all the children inside. I won't be coming this autumn after all, because I've got to begin to work, like poor children did in the olden days. Nobody cares for me any more . . ."

She nods sorrowfully and moves on—through the village and beyond.

She meets many people she doesn't know, and many others who nod to her. But she only looks back at them with the same serious face. A face that is

meant to say: Here I am, all alone, an unfortunate little child, who has been thrown out of her home by hard parents and wicked brothers and sisters.

But no one understands; they all hurry by.

Children run past or stand staring and gaping along the roadside. Some, she notes with disgust, are eating ice-cream. But ice-cream or no ice-cream, they don't pay any attention to her.

At a cross-road she comes to a halt. Not far away, on a little hillock, two fat, well-fed children are guzzling lemonade. All round them lie great sandwiches and buns and bars of chocolate.

Josephine slips down into the ditch and opens her bag. With a misty-eyed gaze she goes through its contents:

"A poor little child am I," something whispers inside her, while she bravely contemplates the muddle inside her bag.

She squeezes a caviar worm on her slice of pancake and then nearly chokes. The pancake ends up in the ditch, which leaves her only the potatoes and toast, and the little that is left in the caviar tube . . .

Then the hunger sets in.

After hunger, she supposes, comes *night*, dark and black and cold. She'll go on walking, pale, and trembling with cold and hunger.

Maybe she won't get any work, for she knows how thin and frail she looks.

And then—then she'll *die*.

That'll serve them right at home! Then they'll be sorry for what they've done. After an experience like that they will have to stop treating her so badly.

Somewhat cheered by this last thought, Josephine closes her bag with its pathetic contents and climbs out of the ditch. But the grass is slippery, and she tumbles straight back into the dirt at the bottom.

With mud dripping from her knees and the fat children on the hillock sniggering at her, she goes off. The last thing she hears is a loud rustling of silver paper. That's the last straw. Now she has had enough. After all, there are limits to one's courage.

But not to disasters, it seems!

The next moment she's lying flat on her face in the road in front of a bicycle.

An old woman jumps down from the bicycle with loud lamentations:

"Oh, my poor dear little child, what a dreadful thing! Didn't you see my bicycle? Oh, dear, oh dear, are you all right? What terrible things can happen in a moment . . ."

Josephine squints up at the old woman, whose blue eyes peer back at her out of a wrinkled face.

It could easily be a witch. In fact, it's the most likely thing. But who cares? One disaster more or less makes no difference, after all she's been through.

Anyway, it would just serve them right at home, if she were spirited away by a witch.

That's why Josephine, without a word, follows the old woman, as she suggests. The old woman lives close by, she says.

They turn off the road, cross a meadow, and turn into a dark winding path; the old woman first, Josephine after her.

The old woman pushes her bicycle, which has a big box behind and a large basket on its handlebars. There is something mysterious about the box and the basket.

The box is full of little holes, out of which come horrible squeakings. Inside the basket one can hear a scratching sound.

The old woman talks and talks. This is to drown out the sounds coming from the box and the basket, Josephine thinks to herself.

But the old woman's words are wise ones. She seems to know just what Josephine wants to hear most of all at this moment: that she's to be *pitied*.

"Oh dearie, dearie me, you poor little lass! All alone, and so little! Now, how can that be? Have they abandoned her, the poor little thing, and so little, too . . ."

Josephine doesn't say a word. But her ears are wide open. The old woman's words are like soft cotton wool round her heart. At last! Someone who's sorry for her! Even if the old woman is a witch, what of it? She's a lot more thoughtful than some people's mothers and fathers, Josephine thinks to herself with bitter satisfaction.

After they have walked a very long way, a glade opens out into the wood. They skirt a green field and come to a cottage on the other side. This must be where the old woman lives.

3

THE OLD WOMAN props her bicycle against her cottage, takes off the box and basket, and sets them down on the ground.

Her arms crossed on her breast, she looks Josephine up and down. Josephine stares back.

At this moment she is convinced that she is looking at a witch. The old crone is thin and boney. Under her dress her elbows are sharp and pointed; so is her chin; her nose is crooked, her eyes like daggers. But her voice is oily-smooth.

"Why don't you say something, my little pet? What's your name, if you've got one?"

Josephine isn't scared. But she hesitates before answering. Hasn't she heard how dangerous it is to tell a witch your name? That's all witches need in order to harm you. But what does she care? It's all the same to her. She's in the witch's power now, anyway.

"Josephine Joandersson," she says boldly.

"That's odd," says the old woman. She sticks her little finger in her mouth and sucks a hollow tooth, staring at Josephine all the while.

"That's odd," she repeats. "I could have sworn you came from the vicarage. Then you aren't the Vicar's youngest?"

"Yes," says Josephine, "I am." Nothing is to be gained by denying it.

Out of the old woman's thin neck comes a creaky laugh. Her shoulders heave. Josephine, fascinated by the sight, just stares and stares; no one she has ever met before laughs like that.

"He-he-he . . . Just teasing an old woman, are you? But no one pulls Granny Lyra's leg that easily! Yes, yes, that's my name, Granny Lyra, and the old man digging out there in the field is my brother, and his name's Justus," she adds, by way of explanation.

Josephine follows the long lean finger. She sees an old man far out in the field, but she says nothing. The old woman goes on:

"Well, and what do they say back home at the vicarage, about you traipsing along the roads like this?"

"Nothing," says Josephine defiantly. "They've thrown me out. Don't want to see me any more."

"Oh dear, oh dear, oh dearie me," the old woman sighs. "That's something I'd never have guessed!"

"Well, they have," says Josephine.

Then the old woman seats herself on her kitchen steps and pulls Josephine down beside her. Out of the pocket of her dress she pulls a bag of sweets and gives Josephine a fistful.

"Just you sit here beside Granny Lyra," she says, "and tell me all about it. That *was* mean of them!" Again she sucks at her tooth. It seems to be a habit of hers and makes her even more fascinating to Josephine. Josephine can see that the hollow tooth is a bit bigger than the others. No one else she knows has quite that sort of tooth.

Josephine stuffs her mouth full of sweets and tells her dismal tale.

No, they don't want her any more. Actually, they probably never did want her. She realizes that now.

Her tongue wags. The old woman asks her cautious questions, rustles her bag, and brings forth more sweets. Yes, indeed! This poor thin child obviously gets beaten. And has her hair pulled. That's why there's so little of it left. Look how fine it is!

The old woman takes a good look. Oh dear, oh dear!—she sighs, again and again.

Josephine fills her mouth again, chews, and tells tales. Yes, now she has to go out into the world and find work; as children used to do in olden times. How is she to get any food, otherwise?

All she owns is in her little bag. She opens it, showing its meagre contents. She hadn't dared take any more: she'd have been spanked.

"Surely they can't be so cruel to someone so small?" says the old woman.

"Oh, yes, they can!" says Josephine. "Even crueller." And she hardly knows what more she can add, to earn her sweets. There are lots left in the old woman's bag. The more she tells, the more sweets Josephine gets. And the more sweets she gets, the more tales she is able to make up.

The witch is obviously interested in her wretched fate. *She is really listening.* That's something they hardly ever do at home. Or if they do, they say she's fibbing.

"They're mean, too," says Josephine, encouraged by yet another handful of sweets. "I never have anything nice to eat, or any toys. My monkey's the only toy I've got, and all my brothers and sisters had him when they were small. Look how ragged he is!"

The old crone sucks her tooth. She twitters.

"Well, you see," she says. "They're too old to have small children. That's something I've always said. And your father, his thoughts float about in the sky . . ."

Josephine doesn't like the old crone's way of talking about Papa-Father. After all, he has nothing at all to do with it. Nor does Mama. It's Agneta who's so silly, though she isn't usually. Really it's all Eric's fault! Josephine is on the point of explaining this, when they are interrupted. Without either of them hearing him, the old woman's brother is suddenly standing there beside them. He is big and dark, and throws a broad shadow over Josephine.

"It looks like rain," he says, scanning the sky. "That's just what we need, after this dry spring we've been having."

The old woman gets up. She too looks up at the sky.

"There's thunder in the air. I've had it in my head all morning. There's a shower coming."

"Get the box from the village?" asks the old fellow. He takes a pinch of snuff but doesn't look at Josephine.

"Yes," says the old woman. And goes over to the box with the holes in it. "Here they are. This child's put everything else out of my mind. She's the Vicar's youngest. They're so nasty to her at home, it's really shocking."

But the old man pays no attention to Josephine.

"Bring me the pliers, so that I can open the box," he says, spitting out a brown stream of snuff.

[23]

The old woman goes off to fetch the pliers. The next moment the lid comes off the box and out come fluffy little chicks running after each other, squeaking.

"They look nice and fat, don't they," says the old man, taking another pinch. "And they'll get fatter still." Then he picks up the box to make off with it, but the old woman stops him. She lifts up the basket that was standing beside it.

"Milly wonders if you'll look after these. They were already so big when she found them, she couldn't do it herself."

The old fellow squirts some snuff.

"Couldn't anyone nearer home get rid of a couple of darn kittens?"

"Ssh, ssh," says the old woman, hushing him, while throwing an uncertain glance at Josephine.

"It's pathetic, that's what it is! Oh well, I suppose I'll have to take care of them."

He goes off with his box, muttering and mumbling to himself.

"Women! What a lot of fuss about nothing!"

Josephine fixes her eyes on the old woman.

"Are there kittens in that basket?"

"N . . . no," answers Granny Lyra. But her glance strays. She puts out her hand, to see if it's raining.

"Upon my word," she says, just to make conversation. "He's right after all! It would be a blessing if it rained after all this drought. Let's go in quickly . . ."

She grabs the basket and thrusts it as far as she can reach under the steps of the porch. From under its lid comes a scratching and whining.

She pushes Josephine before her into the kitchen.

Josephine goes in, saying nothing. But her thoughts go round and round in her head. What a lot of evil there is in the world! What terrible thing is to befall the poor little creatures scratching inside that box? "Take care of them." Does that mean—kill them? It seems like that to her. She throws the old woman a surreptitious glance.

"Now we'll have coffee and fresh buns. And I've

some nice biscuits too, so we'll have a real feast," she says, busying herself and whisking about the kitchen. "If I'd only known that we'd be having such fine visitors in the house, I'd have made a cake, but now it'll have to be some other time."

The rain has started in earnest now, beating against the window-panes. Josephine broods. The old woman chatters.

"You'll come back to Granny Lyra, won't you, when they're nasty to you at home, eh? You're always welcome, you can be sure of that."

Josephine broods. Now she has made up her mind what to do. If only she could get the old woman out of the kitchen . . .

The old crone puts out cups and saucers on the table: for herself, for Josephine, for her brother Justus. The coffee simmers on the stove, giving off sour fumes. That gives Josephine an idea.

"I'm not allowed to drink coffee," she says quietly.

"Stuff and nonsense," says the old woman. "But it isn't your fault. They want to save their coffee beans, I know, I know."

She goes over to the window, sticks her finger in her mouth, sucks her tooth. She stands there a while, looking at the rain.

"It'll pass over soon. I've got lemonade and milk in the cellar under the knoll. If I'd only thought of it

I'd have asked Justus to fetch them in. Now, I suppose I'll have to get them in myself."

Josephine's heart misses a beat. That's just what she'd been hoping for! She places herself next to the old woman at the window. Both watch the rain.

"It's passing over," Josephine says eagerly. "Look, it's not so heavy now!"

"So I see," says the old woman. "You just sit down on the sofa; I'll be back in a jiffy . . ." She throws a black raincoat over her head and sets off. Josephine sees her flap past the window and disappear behind a little knoll.

Quick as lightning Josephine dashes out to the porch steps, crawls underneath, grabs hold of the basket, and rushes off in the opposite direction.

Her heart is in her mouth. Water splashes round her legs; the rain gets worse again; thunder rumbles.

But that's not what frightens Josephine just now. Frightened, panic-stricken, she looks in every direction. Will they follow her? No, there's no sign of them anywhere, neither the old man nor the old woman.

She leaves the field behind her, and plunging into the woods, she is soon swallowed up by the trees. Now no one can see her.

She calms down, takes shelter under a spruce tree. There, in the great calm woods, she lifts the lid off the basket.

Inside is the loveliest sight she has ever seen. Three pairs of blue eyes are looking anxiously up at her. Soft little paws stretch out, and little pink throats whimper.

Three tiny kittens try to get out of the basket.

Gently, Josephine pokes them down again. She tingles all over with happiness.

She has saved them! Three little grey lives!

Now they are hers.

She must go home and get them some cream as quickly as possible. Reluctantly she puts the lid on again.

The rain, no longer pouring down, is just dripping from the trees. But the thunder is coming closer.

That path they'd come by—she and the old woman —where is it? Among all those trees it's hard to find. But in the end she finds it and starts off. The path is endlessly long, even longer now, as she walks on her own. By and by she comes out on to a road. But it's not the right road! It must be another one, for she doesn't recognize it. She remains standing at the roadside with her basket.

Now all her courage begins to drain away. The kittens are whimpering with hunger. The sky is grey, and water is pouring in torrents along the ruts. She, too, is wet and cold.

To cap it all, she discovers that she has left her bag in the old woman's cottage. Well, there's nothing to be done about it now. The kittens are more important than anything else.

Cars drive by, splashing her with mud. If only she knew which direction to walk!

Well, she can't stand here for ever.

Just then a red car comes swishing by in the rain. In all this greyness it looks quite gay.

Making up her mind, she sets off in the same direction as the car. "It knew where it was going," she thinks to herself.

But before she has gone very far, another car

comes to a stop right beside her. Not a red one, but grey, like everything else, of course!

And who should get out of it but Eric, whom Agneta is going to marry.

"My dear Josephine," he says, "what a sight you are! What on earth are you doing here?"

4

How ANNOYING that it is Eric!

Of course it was a good thing someone came by, but it could at least have been someone else. Josephine hasn't much use for Eric. So she decides she's not going to accept a lift from him: nor is she going to *show* him what she thinks. She just stands there sulking, saying nothing.

But then Eric gets out of his car and—without a word—lifts her into the back seat. At the same moment the rain starts again, gushing down in torrents all round the car.

There she sits, her basket on her knees, staring at Eric's dark tousled neck. Funny, there's nothing wrong with his neck. But otherwise he's horrid.

She feels him looking at her in the rear-view mirror. She carefully avoids looking back at him. The next moment the road is covered with water. The rain is like a cascade in front of the car, splashing around the wheels as they drive on.

"You'd have had to swim home, Josephine, if I hadn't come along," says Eric suddenly. "Can you swim?"

Josephine sticks her nose in the air and doesn't reply.

"Whatever are you so sulky about? Maybe you'd like to swim the last bit? We're nearly there."

Josephine doesn't reply. Eric jams on the brakes and turns round.

"Look here—what's the matter with you?"

Josephine looks out of the window.

"You can't stand me, can you?" she hears Eric say.

Josephine makes a face as she meets Eric's eye. She sticks her tongue out at him. *How dare she?*

But Eric knows how to get back at her. He makes a face and sticks out his tongue, looking even more deadly than Josephine.

"No harm having a little facial exercise," he says, when he's finished, rubbing his cheeks. "Happy now?"

Josephine replies with one final scowl. But now her face is tired. So tired, she's on the verge of giggling, but she holds herself back at the last moment. She mustn't forget how horrid Eric is. Though it's a pity.

Because he's fun, too. Now he takes out a bar of chocolate. He offers Josephine a bit.

"I've already had lots of sweets today," Josephine informs him, standing on her dignity. But Eric is not impressed.

"Very well, silly," he says in an offhand way. "Go without, then." He puts a bit in his own mouth. "Besides, this is chocolate, not sweets."

"All right—you can give me a piece, then," says Josephine graciously. "Or two pieces. Thank you."

Both eat silently, but the rain still sings its song in the air outside.

Beside him on the front seat of the car, Eric has a big cardboard box. All of a sudden he points to it and asks Josephine if she knows what's inside.

Naturally, she doesn't.

"A wedding veil," says Eric. Josephine stares at him. Does he already know what has happened to Agneta's veil. And bought a new one? How is it that he isn't angry with her? She blushes.

But Eric goes on:

"This is my mother's wedding veil. Both my mother and my grandmother have worn it, and now my mother wants Agneta to wear it, too. As long as she doesn't feel it's too old-fashioned . . ."

Eric breaks off and looks at Josephine. Bright red in the face, she can't get a word out.

"How funny you look," he says. Then he gives a little sigh. "But I forgot. You don't approve of me," he adds in a troubled tone of voice, "and anyway you're not a bit interested in wedding veils . . ."

Then—at last—Josephine finds her tongue.

"Yes, yes, Eric," she says eagerly. "I am. Of course I'm interested in wedding veils." And before she knows it, she has told Eric the whole story about the butterflies and how Agneta had cried. From beginning to end, exactly as it happened, without adding or omitting the least detail, either.

"My, that *was* a long story!" says Eric, when she has finished. "Well, one really shouldn't touch other people's things without asking. That's something I've found out, too. Believe me. I'll never forget, when I was about your age, making parachutes out of our sitting-room curtains."

"Did you?" says Josephine, giving a little laugh. "Well, I haven't done *that* anyway."

"The curtains were lying in our kitchen, you see, after being washed. Of course, it didn't occur to me that they were curtains. All I saw was the most marvellous parachute silk I could wish for. So I took a pair of scissors, and well . . . you can imagine the rest . . ."

"Hm. Did they spank you?"

"I beat it . . . as fast as I could go."

"Just like me," nods Josephine, and finds she doesn't dislike Eric at all any more.

"But I never knew Agneta had already bought a wedding veil," says Eric afterwards.

"Well, she did. Though of course she can't use it now," says Josephine, guiltily.

"Was that why you ran away, Josephine?"

Josephine grunts non-committally.

Suddenly she sits up and seizes her basket.

"We have to hurry, Eric," she says. "Do you know what I've got in here?"

"Well, I did notice a funny sort of scratching noise . . ."

Then Josephine opens the lid and tells him all

about her rescue exploit. And now she exaggerates quite a bit, adding things here and leaving things out there. But the fact remains: *it was she who rescued the kittens.*

"Well done, Josephine!" cries Eric with feeling. And then she knows they are friends. She takes one of the tiny kittens out of the basket and hands it to him.

"You can have it, Eric. You and Agneta."

The kitten closes his eyes, beats the air with his paws, and even makes a pathetic attempt to arch its back.

"He doesn't want that," says Eric, laughing. "He wants to stay with his brother and sister."

"*He has to go with you,*" Josephine decrees.

But Eric just gives the kitten a sympathetic pat.

"It'd be cruel to take him to town, where Agneta and I are going to live. Can't you look after him for us?"

"If you come and see him often . . ."

"Every week, I promise."

"Very well, then."

Josephine places the whimpering kitten back in the basket, and Eric starts up the car.

But just as they are about to turn into the driveway of the vicarage, he looks at Josephine in the mirror and says:

[36]

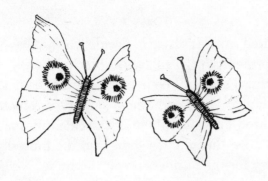

"Do you know what I'd like to have from you?"

"What?"

"One of those butterflies that you made out of the wedding veil."

Josephine's ears go all red with pleasure.

"I've only got to sew the eyes on them," she says.

In the evening, when all is well again, when Josephine has been given permission to keep the kittens and has fed them with cream, when she is clean and tidy and forgiven for disappearing and giving everyone such a fright—yes, when peace and quiet have been restored and joy reigns again, then she takes out the butterflies and sits down to sew on their eyes.

Everyone is to have a butterfly—everyone in the whole house. And each butterfly must have different coloured eyes.

She sits up in bed, surrounded by tufts of bright

coloured wool. It's hard to decide who's to have what.

But the first is given eyes as blue as the sky. That's for Papa-Father, of course. What other colour could possibly do for Papa-Father's butterfly? Agneta's are given red eyes. Josephine has decided on that after some deep thought. To show that the butterfly, too, is sorry for the business about the bride's veil. After all, you do get red eyes from crying.

Eric's is given green: green eyes go so well with the red ones on Agneta's butterfly.

But when Josephine comes to sew eyes on her own butterfly, she can't make up her mind. First she makes a blue one, then a red one, to try them out. A heavenly eye and a weeping eye, she thinks. But then she pulls out the weeping eye, and sews on a green one instead.

One eye for heaven. One for earth.

Yes, that's how she wants it.

5

IT SOMETIMES happens that Papa-Father goes for a walk with Josephine.

Then he tells her about nature. Tells her about it in his own way—little stories, not easily forgotten.

But today Papa-Father is unhappy—and something unhappier than that doesn't exist, because no one can be so unhappy as he.

His unhappiness makes itself felt throughout the whole vicarage. You know it immediately when you wake up, just the way you can tell the sky is grey before you even see it.

It is as if everything stands still. Everything is heavy and silent—just waiting for him to be happy again.

The furniture looks gloomy. The curtains hardly

dare breathe. All the door handles hang down. It's the same in the garden. The shadows look grey instead of blue. The wind sighs so sadly in the grass, even the birds seem anxious.

Wherever you go sadness reigns.

Papa-Father's hair, which usually stands straight up like a bristly brush, lies flat, and his face is full of wrinkles.

That's the sort of day it is today.

Papa-Father is sitting in his study, his head in his hands. Not a sound is heard. Josephine is playing silently outside his window.

It is morning. A thunder shower has just moistened the grass and leaves. But the sky brightens, and suddenly a brilliant rainbow appears over the vicarage. To disturb Papa-Father is something unheard of—but a rainbow, after all, is a rainbow. Maybe it can comfort him!

Josephine clambers up on to the garden bench under his window and knocks softly at the pane. She knocks twice—then he opens.

"How does one comfort papas?" she whispers, shyly.

"How does one comfort little girls?" he replies.

Then Josephine points at the rainbow. And Papa-Father looks in that direction. Some of his wrinkles disappear, or so she fancies. Then she says:

"Let's go for a rainbow walk."

Breathlessly, she waits . . .

"All right, Josephine, let's," he replies at last. And he definitely loses another wrinkle. Soon they are on their way.

Beneath the trees in the avenue, across the churchyard, out into the meadow. And all the while the rainbow shines down on them.

When one takes a walk with Papa-Father one has to wait until he starts talking. Sometimes it takes a long time before that happens. Sometimes he says nothing at all. But it doesn't matter.

Josephine knows how to talk to him even so. Their feet talk to each other as they walk. As the gravel crackles and crunches underfoot in the avenue, as the sand rustles on the path in the churchyard, and as the grass swishes about their feet in the meadow, then they are talking to each other.

"So—you really do care for me just a little?" rustle Papa-Father's feet questioningly in the grass.

"Yes, I do, I do," Josephine's feet eagerly rustle back their answer. "Do you care about me?"

"That's something you can be sure of," is the reassuring answer from the large feet in the black galoshes.

"Will we have a story today?" Josephine's ask cautiously.

"Maybe, maybe not, may . . ." Papa-Father's reply promisingly.

Soon the weather turns fine. The rainbow shimmers; the sun is on the way.

Suddenly Papa-Father stops under a birch tree. He stands looking into a raindrop, which is clinging to the outermost tip of a branch.

"Do you see?"

Josephine, too, looks into the raindrop and sees everything reflected in it as clearly as in the mirror on the wall at home. Only much smaller. She can see the whole church in it, but it is smaller than anything else in the whole world.

And in the raindrop the church tower is topsy-turvy, though in reality it's the right way up. Other little raindrops are sitting on the twigs—and in each and every one of them the church tower is pointing downwards. What fun!

Yes, says Papa-Father. And begins talking. So that Josephine knows at once there's going to be a story. She can hear it in his voice. It's a story about raindrops, and Josephine listens breathlessly, knowing nothing about their strange life.

"A raindrop is a tiny creature born high high up in the air, on the rainbow perhaps, perhaps even higher, higher perhaps than the eye can see—no one can know for sure," Papa-Father begins. And Josephine looks as high up into the air as she can, while he goes on: "As soon as the tiny drop is big enough, it has to leave home, and go out into the air. It begins to fall."

"How awful for it," says Josephine.

"Not at all," Papa-Father replies. "On the contrary. Falling feels wonderful for a raindrop, because that is what raindrops are meant to do. The whole rainbow is made up of millions and millions of tiny falling raindrops, who reflect the heavens as they fall."

"Do they reflect heaven upside-down, too?" Josephine wonders.

"Yes, upside-down, we might say. But if one thinks about it, there's not so much difference between up and down as one might at first imagine. We say the raindrops are falling, but they themselves think they're flying. We say we fly up to heaven. And the raindrops say they are flying up to the earth. The earth is their heaven."

"They've a funny sort of heaven," says Josephine, thoughtfully.

"But beautiful as well," says Papa-Father. "We must do what we can to make the earth a nice heaven for the raindrops, don't you think?"

"Of course. Do raindrops become angels when they come to their heaven?"

"In a way," says Papa-Father. "They become angels in a raindrop's fashion, one might say."

Then Papa-Father says not a single raindrop falls in vain. For every one that falls, a blade of grass grows, or a flower blooms, he goes on, and this is what the raindrops long for and dream about as they hang trembling on the outermost tip of a branch, waiting. Though they haven't the faintest idea of it themselves, no more than we have any idea of what happens to us in heaven.

"How can you long for something you don't know about?" asks Josephine.

"Yes, how? Tell me that, Josephine!" And Josephine gets a notion that this is something Papa-Father, too, wonders a lot about. But now he looks cheerful again, his hair is standing upright, and there are no more wrinkles in his face.

"Shall we help the raindrops?" asks Josephine, who wants to shake the birch tree. But Papa-Father stops her.

"Oh, no!" he says. "The wind will help them. Just wait and see!"

And by and by a faint breeze blows through the tree, so that all the tiny drops fall in glittering rainbows to the ground.

6

Now SUMMER has really come in earnest; the sun is shining from morning to evening. Day after day there's not a cloud in the sky.

"It's lovely," thinks Josephine. But all the grown-ups shake their heads and say it's altogether too dry. What's needed is rain, lots of rain. Not a drop has fallen since that day Josephine went for a rainbow walk with Papa-Father. And that was weeks and weeks ago. So much has happened since then. So much . . .

Agneta has married Eric and moved to town.

At the wedding Josephine was bridesmaid and held Agneta's bouquet. To bring Agneta luck she smuggled in three ladybirds and a huge money-spider among the lilies-of-the-valley.

And they did, though Agneta didn't much appre-

ciate the spider. He didn't know how to behave himself, but hopped from the bouquet on to Agneta. He moved at a terrific speed and tickled as he ran. Anyway, he appeared in the wedding photo! You can see him on the veil, right by her neck. Josephine is enormously proud of that.

For days before the wedding there were any amount of people at the vicarage, all her brothers and sisters and their children and many, many more. Then the wedding was all over, Agneta and Eric had gone, and it seemed very empty after that.

Yes, how empty it was . . .

For a whole month Agneta and Eric didn't once come to visit, for they'd gone on a long journey. But now they've started to come and see to their kitten, as they promised. And though she doesn't live at home any more, Agneta often comes over alone.

It's a good thing Josephine has the kittens, or she'd be even more lonely. They're quite big now. One of them even tried to attack some birds. Now all three of them have to wear bells round their necks, so that the birds will hear them.

Sometimes Josephine is allowed to swim in the lake, when Mama has time to come with her. She picks flowers and runs errands in the village.

There are lots of children in the village, but they won't play with her. They just run past her, as if she were clear as air. Or else they stand in little groups and stare at her as if she were a monster.

She understands: she doesn't *know* enough to be allowed to be with them. They know so many more games. They can ride bicycles and play hopscotch and marbles. Once Josephine joined in their hop-scotch, but of course she did everything wrong and that was the end of that. Another time she was given a whole bag of marbles to go and play with the vil-lage children, but she lost them all immediately, not knowing how to play. When her marbles had gone, no one would play with her any more.

They must know everything, the village children. It'll be exciting to begin school. Then perhaps she'll learn, too. They lick ices and chew gum; and they always have money, which Josephine hasn't.

At home no one has much time to be with her.

It's been ages since Papa-Father and she went for a walk. It's his busiest time now. There are weddings almost every day, and he has to teach all the big boys and girls who are to be confirmed in the sum-mer. Then, too, there are funerals! Yes, people die in the summer, also, though there can't be much fun in that, thinks Josephine. If one has to die, at least it ought to be in the winter, when it's dark outside and the weather is bad.

Old Mandy is up to her ears with work in the kitchen. Yet she is the one who has the most time for Josephine.

Mama has hardly any time at all. She always has a terrible lot to do and remember; and she is so forgetful.

She ties funny little knots in her hankies and dusters, but then forgets everything just the same; and her bun of fair hair bobs anxiously up and down at her neck. Josephine helps her tie the knots, but sometimes everything gets into a frightful muddle for both of them, and then Mama puts her hand to her forehead and laughs:

"Oh dear, I'm at my wits' end, Josephine."

Mama flies through the rooms. She wears slim shiny shoes that one can't help admiring, for quieter shoes, or quieter feet, don't exist; they never stamp. Absolutely silent, they move faster than the wind. They can even go across the gravel in the avenue without being heard! Josephine's feet could never carry on the same conversations with Mama's feet as they do with Papa-Father's.

On the other hand, one never has to hold one's tongue when one is with Mama. One can always talk to her; for her part, she talks as quickly as she walks,

and almost as quietly. But Mama is nearly always tired. Often, when she sits down to read or do some sewing, she just drops off to sleep. That's why her table-cloth for the bazaar never gets finished.

Every year there is a bazaar in the autumn and another in the spring; and each time Mama begins on her table-cloth a week before. Once Josephine helped her, but that didn't do much good. Now six bazaars have come and gone, the table-cloths weren't ready, and this upsets Mama ever so much.

The days pass—long lovely days—but Josephine doesn't always know what to do with them. Sometimes she's a trifle bored, there's no denying it. And that's why she's so happy when Mama says one morning:

"Today Anton Godmarsson's coming. He's our new gardener."

Josephine says she thinks Godmarsson's a funny name, though it suits a vicarage garden.

"Yes, maybe it does," says Mama. "Godmarsson is a good fellow and knows his business, though he looks a bit odd. Remember, be nice to him, because he needs it."

"In what way does he look odd?" Josephine wonders.

"You'll be able to see for yourself," Mama replies, being in a hurry. "But remember what I'm saying! You mustn't giggle at him, or be silly, like little girls sometimes are. Do you hear?"

"Hm," mumbles Josephine, hurt. Mama's always afraid she'll do something silly. Always saying that.

"When's he coming?" asks Josephine, just as Mama disappears.

"I don't know, some time during the day, I suppose," Mama replies. And runs off.

7

JOSEPHINE is more than a little curious about Anton Godmarsson. That's why she goes down to the village to see if perhaps he's on the 10 o'clock bus. She gets there in good time, with quite a while to wait before the bus arrives, so she takes a stroll down the village street. It's warm; the children are eating ice-cream and bathing in the brook that runs through the village. An old woman is walloping her washing on the bridge over the stream. Here and there people are drinking coffee and lemonade in their gardens. But since she hardly knows them, Josephine isn't offered any. They just nod to her, and she nods back. There's not much to do in the village today.

At last the bus comes. Josephine runs to the bus

stop. But Anton Godmarsson isn't on it. Only one old woman gets off. The bus sets off again. The old woman limps away with her shopping basket.

Then Josephine's heart jumps into her throat. It's . . . it's the old woman from the wood! Granny Lyra, as she's called! Josephine hasn't seen her since that day, but she's thought about her a lot. Really, she was quite a nice old lady, thinks Josephine, remembering all the sweets she'd been given . . .

Mandy left the basket the kittens were in at the shop, so the old woman has had that back. But Josephine's bag is still up there in the woods. The old woman comes nearer. She hasn't caught sight of Josephine yet. Maybe she doesn't even recognize her. Josephine doesn't really know what she wants. Her heart thuds: Does she want the old woman to see her? Or to walk past?

Josephine remembers when Mandy told her the story of Hansel and Gretel and the old witch in the gingerbread house who gave them so much food, just to eat them up afterwards, then Josephine saw this old woman in her mind's eye. So nasty, to think such a thing. Josephine feels badly about it, and that's why her heart is thudding as it is.

Then the old woman stops.

"Why, if it isn't the Vicar's little daughter! My, my, what a long time it's been!" She goes up to Josephine, who is very embarrassed.

"How quick you were to run off with those kittens —I was quite terrified, with the thunder and all. But we won't talk any more about that. It's nice to see you, Miss."

"Yes," says Josephine and can't get out another word.

"It's so hot today! Had an ice-cream cone yet?"

"No," says Josephine.

"Then Granny Lyra'll give you one. We'll go to the shop at once."

There are several children in the shop, and Josephine gets the biggest size of cone there is. That'll teach them! She's not as stupid as they imagine! The old woman buys a bag of sweets, too.

"Anything else you'd fancy?" she asks Josephine.

Josephine's cheeks turn red. She can't really say it, can she?

"Well . . . yes, thanks," she stammers out at last, "a . . . some chewing-gum . . . maybe . . . though . . ."

Immediately she gets two packages. And the children hanging about the counter notice that, too. Her nose in the air, Josephine leaves the shop.

Outside stands the old woman's bicycle. Now she's going to ride home. But then she remembers:

"What about your little bag? You left it with me. I've thought to myself so many times I ought to take it up to the vicarage, but there's always so much to carry when one has to go down to the village. And Justus, my brother, he's so awfully lazy and useless, you can't get him to do anything."

"I can fetch the bag myself," says Josephine.

"Why don't you come for it now?" asks the old woman. "You can sit up behind me on my bicycle, and I'll give you a ride back afterwards."

Why not? Josephine has nothing to do, and no one knows when the new gardener is going to turn up. So she decides to go.

"Then I'll buy a cake at the baker's, and we can have our little feast this time instead."

Soon Josephine is sitting on the back of the old woman's bicycle with a cake box bobbing up and down on her knee. She isn't afraid of the old woman any more. Granny can't be a witch if she buys so many sweets.

When they get there, Granny lays the table for a feast in the garden bower. Brother Justus isn't at home.

"They had no big cake today, so I got some little ones instead. They'll do just as well. You can have as many as you like."

First Josephine takes a green one with marzipan on it.

"Well, and how are things at home now?" asks the old woman, as she pours out some lemonade. "Better?"

"Yes," says Josephine. "Anton Godmarsson's coming to us today."

"*Who* did you say?"

"Anton Godmarsson, our new gardener."

"*Lord!*" exclaims the old woman, sitting down heavily on the bench. "They can't be in their right minds up there. Is he really coming to you?"

"He knows his job, Mama says," Josephine replies, her mouth full.

The old woman sucks her tooth—just like the last time, Josephine remembers.

"He certainly isn't fond of work," she says flatly. "That he isn't."

The green cake has come to an end. It was lovely, and there are many more left. Josephine looks at the plate.

"Find them to your taste, eh?" says the old woman, pleased, putting another with chocolate on it in front of Josephine. Then she asks whether Josephine has had any food today, and in her hurry Josephine forgets the porridge she had for breakfast, and answers "no".

"So they send you out on an empty stomach, do they? Poor little mite! How can they be so cruel?"

Josephine has her mouth full of chocolate cream and her eyes glued to the plate of cakes in front of her. Which shall she have next?

"Are they really so cruel to you?" the voice beside her repeats.

"Yes, well, sometimes," says Josephine, deciding on the cream cake. She takes it, and another big glass of fruit juice. It is strawberry juice, marvellous.

"Really? Are they so cruel to you? Well, I can just believe it."

Josephine makes short work of the cream cake and a butterscotch one, too. She lends only half an ear to the old woman. But, she thinks to herself, she's a nice kind old woman. Talks a bit too much, doesn't give me time to answer all her questions, but she's really quite nice. Like a granny, almost.

Josephine has heard about other children who have grannies. From a granny one can get almost anything. But she hasn't got one. Hers is dead. But supposing . . . She looks at the old woman and makes up her mind.

"Would you like to be my granny? I haven't got one, she's dead."

To begin with, all that is heard by way of an answer is a violent sucking at the tooth; but then the old woman says she would.

"Granny Lyra," she says. "That's me, is it? Very well, my pretty one, it suits me, it does."

Then Josephine asks: "Haven't you any husband?" It crosses her mind that she might be able to get a grandpa into the bargain.

"No. I haven't been married, you see. All I've got is my brother Justus," the old woman replies; and Josephine thinks to herself that she may as well do without a grandpa, rather than take one that kills kittens—though of course she doesn't say so.

The old woman seems very happy to have become a grandmother. She chats and chats:

"Then you can come to Granny Lyra as often as you like. You can eat as much as you like here, and get plump and pretty. It's a shame to see how thin you are. Simple folks like us aren't stingy. No one ever goes hungry from Judith Lyra's table. What sort of things do you eat at your home?"

"Fish-cakes," Josephine says, for they are her favourites.

"Call that food?" sighs the old woman. "What, no meat?"

But Josephine has just got hold of the cake she was keeping until last, a meringue, and with one's mouth full of meringue one doesn't want to talk about meat. So she doesn't reply, and the old woman puts a bag of sweets on the table in front of her. With a firm hand she pats Josephine:

"Poor little dear," she says, "just tell Granny Lyra. You do have a hard time of it, don't you? Tell me . . ."

At first Josephine understands nothing. What is there to tell? Then she realizes that Granny Lyra wants to know if she gets many sweets at home. She shakes her head.

"And what about clothes? Don't they ever give you anything new to wear?"

"Oh yes," Josephine explains that she gets second-hand clothes from her brother Charles's children, since she is their aunt—yes, even though they *are* bigger than she is and have begun school already! But then Granny Lyra asks whether they ever *buy* her anything?

"We can't afford it," says Josephine, which is the

simple truth, as Mama is always telling her. Then Granny Lyra is really terribly sorry for Josephine and tips a great heap of sweets on to her plate.

"So, it's like that, is it? They can't afford it, can't they? And the little ones have to suffer."

Josephine gobbles the sweets and Granny Lyra pours her coffee into her saucer, sucking it noisily into her mouth, making long gurgling noises.

Suddenly Josephine feels terribly full. She gets a little pain in her stomach. Not one more sweet will go down.

And Granny Lyra at once explains:

"You always get a pain in your tummy when you're not used to food. It's because they starve you, poor little mite. They don't know what children need."

She sets Josephine on her knee, and there she remains, feeling more and more queasy. She understands how sorry she ought to be for herself, even though she hadn't ever realized it before. All the forgotten injustices pop up: the time she was spanked for eating all the honey in the larder; the time when she tried to clamber up to the treacle tin and fell into the egg basket; when she . . . ugh, what a lot of tragedies have been hers, now that she comes to think of it! And she tells them all to Granny Lyra, who asks questions and consoles her, while her tummy aches.

But when Josephine can't find any more tales to tell, Granny Lyra says:

"Yes, yes, yours is a hard life, my dear. But now Granny Lyra's going to give you a doll, that she is. A lovely big doll with hair."

At once Josephine forgets her tummy-ache.

"One that can shut her eyes?" she asks breathlessly.

"Yes, I'm sure she'll be able to do that."

Josephine ponders. There are dolls that can eat and go to the lavatory—so she's heard.

"Will mine be able to?" she asks.

"We'll see. You'll have to wait until I've been to town."

Well, of course. Josephine has no objection to waiting. She ponders again.

"And there are some that can walk, too," she says, after a moment, "but I don't want one of them."

"Oh? Why not?"

"Because it would be too much to ask, wouldn't it?" says Josephine, trying her luck.

"We'll see, we'll see," answers the old woman.

Josephine looks dreamily in front of her.

"And there are some that can talk, too," she says, mostly to herself.

"We'll see, we'll see," the old woman says again.

Then she gives Josephine a lift almost the whole

way home. And while she's cycling along she carefully points out the way to Josephine, so that she can walk over by herself. It's not far at all, and wild raspberries, big as eggs, and wild strawberries as large as garden ones are growing all along the last stretch. The raspberries will soon be ripe.

Yes, the way to Granny Lyra is full of treats; Josephine can see that.

8

JOSEPHINE runs into the kitchen and tells Mandy all about Granny Lyra and the doll she's going to get. And the cakes and the ice-cream and sweets. But not about the chewing-gum that still lies unopened in the pocket of her dress. She's going to keep that until she has to go down to the village, so that the village children can see her chewing it. Anyway, she knows what they think about chewing-gum here at home; that's something to keep quiet about.

"Granny Lyra's so nice, so nice," Josephine concludes. "If you only knew, Mandy . . ."

"That's as may be . . ." says Mandy, rolling her dough hard with the rolling-pin.

Just then Mama comes in, and Josephine tells her,

too, all about how nice and kind Granny Lyra is.

"And she let me eat as much as I liked, and the doll can blink and eat and go to the toilet and maybe even walk."

"I've never heard such a thing," says Mama, turning to Mandy. "She really must be kind, Miss Lyra."

Mandy doesn't reply.

"Yes," Josephine assures her, "there's no one kinder in the whole world."

"But must you really call her 'Granny'?" asks Mama. "Can't you call her Auntie Judith?"

"No," says Josephine. "I want a granny, too."

"Of course," says Mama. "I merely thought . . ."

But then she breaks off short and looks at Mandy, who slaps the dough angrily on the rolling-board.

"What's the matter, Mandy?"

Mandy gives the dough another resounding smack. Her face is bright red.

"That's going too far," she says, her eyes flashing. "What a lot of things one has to listen to, before one's ears fall off!"

"But Mandy . . ."

"Granny Lyra indeed! *Harpy*, I'd call her. She certainly knows how to play sweet music, anyway!"

"But Mandy," Mama reproaches her. "Anyone can see she's a kind-hearted decent old soul."

"Hm," says Mandy and attacks the dough again.

[64]

"But a harpy, just the same."

Mama shakes her head and leads Josephine out of the kitchen.

"If you ask me," she says, in a troubled tone of voice, laughing a little, "Mandy's jealous. Dear old Mandy, that's something I'd *never* have thought of her! You'd better go back and give her a real hug, Josephine."

And Josephine does, with the best will in the world; but Mandy acts just as she did before. Not until Josephine is on the point of leaving the kitchen does she give her a little pat on the cheek, saying:

"Don't be cross with old Mandy, Josephine."

No, she isn't "cross", as Mandy puts it. She gives Mandy another hug:

"I know!" she says, delighted with her own idea. "You can be my *other* granny, Mandy! I haven't even got one granny, have I?"

Then Mandy shakes her head violently, even though she doesn't look cross any longer.

"Thank you, thank you, Josephine," she replies firmly, "but I'm quite happy to be old Mandy. It has done well enough until now, and it'll do for the future."

"Yes," says Josephine, thoughtfully. "I suppose it's better like that, because if you became my granny, Mandy, then I wouldn't have any Mandy, would I?

And I'd never find another Mandy!" Then Mandy
gives her an enormous hug, pushes her out of the
kitchen, and blows her nose.

"Now you get on out into the sunshine and don't
stand here gossiping with silly old women," she says,
in her usual rough way.

"Has Anton Godmarsson arrived?" Josephine asks,
in the doorway.

"No, we haven't seen him yet. Now it's so late that
he probably isn't coming until tomorrow."

Josephine still lingers.

"Does he like to work?" she asks, after a moment.
Granny Lyra had said he didn't—although she
doesn't tell Mandy that.

Mandy gives her a stare.

"Lord bless us, listen to the child talk!" she says. "How should I know? I've never met him, but I'm sure he can work as well as anyone else. Now, come on, out into the sunshine, Miss!"

Josephine grabs a bit of dough and is gone like an arrow.

9

IT'S BLAZING hot today. Mama hasn't time to take Josephine down to the lake and swim. No one has time for her.

Anton Godmarsson came this morning, while she was still asleep. Then he vanished again to buy some plants. That's why she still hasn't had a glimpse of him, and it'll be some time before he gets back, says Mandy.

What on earth can she do today?

Go to the village, maybe, and chew gum? That will show the other children!

First she must practise her chewing in front of the mirror. The chewing-gum is still lying in its pretty wrappers. It is rather hard, and smells nice. Now she

pops a piece into her mouth and goes over to the
mirror. That looks about right—though she must
make bigger movements with her jaw. Like that! And
smack her lips a bit, as if she'd been doing it all her
life.

No trouble at all! Now her mouth smacks and
smacks as she chews. Josephine isn't behind the
times, whatever they may think down in the village!

If only she didn't look so . . . what's that word
they're always using for her? Yes, *old-fashioned*,
that's what they call her.

"That old-fashioned kid'd better stay out of it,"
that's what they always say.

Josephine stares at herself in the mirror. Hm. It's
true. She looks . . . old-fashioned. Why? Because
everything else in the vicarage is old-fashioned.

Granny Lyra's right. They never buy anything
new here at home. If anyone needs anything, they
have only to go up into the attic and look around—
there's always something they can use. Something
old-fashioned, of course. Anyone can see that the
dress Josephine is wearing wasn't bought for her, but
was *passed on* to her!

Yes, yes, she understands only too well. Children
with short hair and short, wide skirts don't play with
someone who looks the way she does. Her hair is
long, her dress, too. Why hadn't she thought of it

before? That's why the village children don't want to have anything to do with her!

But . . . maybe she can do something about it. Maybe she can smarten herself up. Well, at least she can try . . .

Josephine slips quietly into her mother's room. There's the sewing table, and on the sewing table lies a pair of scissors, a big pair of scissors. She takes them.

And glides noiselessly out again.

First she must take off her dress. Then it'll be the easiest thing in the world to shorten it. She cuts off a broad strip all round. Now the skirt is as short as can be. She puts it on again. Well . . . it certainly doesn't look old-fashioned any more.

And her hair . . . that's easy to cut, too. It just drops off as soon as she puts the scissors to it. It's fun, cutting hair. Though it's difficult behind, because you can't see that part of yourself in the mirror. Once or twice she snips her ears and the collar of her dress. The collar goes to pieces, but her ears are still there. That's the main thing.

Now she's ready.

Pleased with herself, Josephine looks in the mirror. Her hair could have been still shorter, but now she's in a hurry to be off. Anyway, it's better than before.

Though her dress and her hair do look a bit untidy . . . But what does that matter? Down in the village, the untidier the child, the more she has to say about things. Josephine has noticed that. And it's the untidy ones who wouldn't play with her. Now, perhaps, it'll be another story!

The untidy children usually wear a bold, dangerous air. And Josephine? Doesn't she, now? Yes, she thinks so . . .

She runs all the way down to the village. First to the shop, because that's where the village children usually gather to play.

How hot it is today! By the time she arrives, her clothes are sticking to her. But her throat's so dry it scorches.

When your mouth is dry the chewing-gum sticks

to it. She chews and chews until her jaws ache, but she can't produce so much as one sound. What luck no one seems to be around. Because outside the shop the street is empty as can be. Through the windows Josephine can see it's empty inside too.

A strange stillness hangs over the village. Everyone is taking a nap in the heat. From under the awnings in people's gardens comes the faint clink of glasses and cups. Behind a bush a newspaper rustles, and a snore rises from a hammock. Otherwise there's not a sound.

But what about the children? Just because it's hot they don't usually run away and hide! Josephine races round the village, breathless and disappointed.

At last she meets an old man. He looks at her and laughs:

"If you're taking the bus to the bathing beach you'd better hurry," he says.

"The bus?"

"Yes, haven't you heard? All the children in the village are taking a bus down to the lake today. They're having swimming lessons there. The bus is standing outside the school. Doesn't cost anything. You can catch it if you run."

And away she goes.

Long before she gets there she catches sight of the bus, a big yellow one with gay streamers strung across the front. The children are running round it, waving gaily-coloured bathing towels and swimsuits. Mothers are bustling about, carrying picnic baskets and beach bags.

Cautiously, Josephine approaches.

At first, no one notices her. Everyone is busy with his or her own affairs. But now all the children are sitting inside the bus. Mothers are jostling one another around the door, shouting:

"Now remember! Don't go too far out!"

"Don't stay in too long!"

"Remember to obey the teacher!"

Josephine edges closer, chewing her gum as boldly as she possibly can. She leans against a tree and tries to look debonair.

Then, suddenly, the uproar in the bus dies down, all the waving arms and hands are paralysed. The bits of motherly advice fall on deaf ears.

The children have caught sight of Josephine. All eyes gaze at her, and she boldly stares back into as many as she can. But it's no good.

First, scattered giggles are heard: then a storm of merriment breaks loose.

"Look! Just look at that kid! She's mad, she must be!"

At that moment the bus starts. All its occupants screech and howl and wave at her. Frozen, Josephine stands under the tree. The chewing-gum lies like a lump of stone on her tongue. A little further down, in her throat, is another lump.

Without looking where she's going, she rushes away.

10

As JOSEPHINE runs home from the village, she has only one thought in her head: *she is going to swim.*

All the others are allowed to: they're allowed to take the bus without their mothers, she has seen it with her own eyes. So why can't she swim without her mother?

She doesn't dare go to the lake. But there's another place. A little stream called Angel Brook. She isn't allowed to go there, because little children can get drowned in it and become angels—at least that's what people say. Not that just anyone can become an angel. Papa-Father says that it's only good and obedient children who can, and Josephine doesn't feel particularly good or obedient just now, with chewing-gum in her mouth, and her hair and dress cut short!

But there can't be much danger in taking a little dip in Angel Brook. Though for safety's sake she thinks she'll do one more naughty thing—something which, ordinarily, she wouldn't dream of doing.

She'll eat some of the cherries on the cherry tree in the garden. No one's allowed to touch that tree, and no one does; for Mandy makes jam from the fruit, and no one wants to miss that, Josephine least of all.

But today she has other things in her head.

It's a good thing the tree exists. Papa-Father has told her about a girl called Eve. She was the first girl on earth. Apparently she didn't want to become an angel, either, and that's why she ate the forbidden fruit—though *that* tree had apples, which were probably saved to make apple pie for the Almighty. She offered some to a boy called Adam, too. After that there was no danger of them becoming angels. In fact, God the Father got so cross with them that he didn't ever want to see them again. And that's why Josephine eats as many of the cherries as she can possibly hold. They taste good, too, and the more she eats, the less chance she has of becoming an angel.

Finally, she can't reach another single cherry. But she's had plenty. Now she can go and take a little dip in Angel Brook.

The stream runs along the edge of the woods. It

separates Bell Meadow from the woods beyond. It is wide and roars between its banks. You can hear it from far off.

What a lovely day!

The sun is shining, the grass tickles her toes. In her mouth lingers a sweet taste of cherries. If you have any troubles, this is the place to forget all about them. Josephine doesn't think any more about what happened down in the village. Stupid, stuck-up children! They are conceited just because they are allowed to go and swim! What of it? She's going swimming, too, all alone. She's every bit as good as they.

The closer she comes to Angel Brook, the happier she feels. The water chuckles and rushes merrily along. It swirls and gurgles.

The water is dark brown, like dark beer, yet quite transparent. White stones are shining at the bottom. From all sides the stream draws water to itself, forming myriad little whirling circles. It splashes and foams and silvery rings float on the surface. What fun!

No danger here!

Josephine wanders along the bank, trying to find a good place for a dip. Over there is a little wooden bridge. If you cross it you find yourself in the dark woods. Beneath the bridge are some big stones, which the water rushes and jumps over, flinging itself at them so that the foam leaps up into the air. You can't swim there. But just below it the brook broadens out and flows more calmly. *There!*

Josephine dips one toe into the water—it's icy. Out comes her toe!

Swimming is something you have to take gradually. After all, she has the whole day ahead of her. No one says she has to go in right away. First she'll undress and sun-bathe for a while. But before that she'll play ducks and drakes. Eric has taught her how. The little stones skid over the water in the funniest way, and the sun glitters in the spray. What a day!

A short distance from the bank is a grassy little island. With a skip and a jump Josephine reaches it. Now she's a little way out into the stream. The water swirls round the grassy islet. When she kneels down she can stick her fingers into the little holes where the water spins round and round. It tickles, in the funniest way. It's cold, too, but the water chuckles, calm and friendly.

Over there is a lovely deep hole. Josephine reaches into it and slips off her little island . . . *splash* . . .

There she lies in the friendly water, the cold water! Poor Josephine! She sinks like a stone to the bottom, like a stone among all the other little stones. And on the surface there's only a ring, a trifle bigger than all the other rings. For a moment not a sound is heard. Just the stream, roaring, the woods sighing.

Then comes a sound of wild splashing, a scream, a howl of terror that frightens all the birds away. It's Josephine, fighting for her life in Angel Brook. She's alone and drowning.

The stream is determined. It's been so long since it has had any children to make angels of that it's even willing to settle for Josephine. The brook is like a pack of hungry wolves in a fairy tale; it has to make do with whatever it can get . . .

Then . . . a sound of heavy footsteps! A deep voice booms across the meadow! Josephine sees an immense shadow approaching. She closes her eyes and lets out a howl.

When she feels someone grasping her, she struggles like a mad thing with her arms and legs, splashing and fighting and screaming. She struggles until she can't struggle any more.

Then he has her in his power.

He holds her tight in his huge arms. He lifts her straight out of the water and walks with heavy steps. Josephine knows who it is. She's known all along. She needed only to see his shadow.

It's Old Man God.

Now she hears his muffled voice above her head:

"What a peculiar little brat, not wanting to come out of the water! Proper little savage, I'd say."

Josephine lies stiff and unmoving in his arms.

Then, cautiously, she opens one eye. He looks just like his pictures. Old and tired, white hair, white beard. He has a sky-blue shirt, too, and pale blue eyes. It's certainly easy to recognize him.

He looks kind, as God should. Yet she'd much sooner stay at home in the vicarage, where she knows everyone. For she doesn't know a single angel.

And since she isn't even allowed to play with the village children, she certainly won't be allowed to play with the angels.

Josephine opens another eye and looks at him.

"I'm not worth taking," she sobs.

"Oh, no?" he answers, marching on in his great boots.

"I . . . I don't want to be an angel, I'm not the right sort," she tries again.

"No?"

"No, and I'm not good company for angels, either," says Josephine. "Heaven will be full of *bad* angels if I get there."

Josephine does her utmost to persuade him; her voice is respectful and sounds convincing, she thinks. And he seems to be listening to her.

"I've eaten from the forbidden cherry tree, too," she lets him know, finally. "Lots and lots of cherries!"

Now they're right in the middle of Bell Meadow. Over there she can see the church and its bell-tower. So close to home, and yet so far away!

Suddenly she hears the church bells ringing. Never have they sounded so fateful to Josephine. She holds her breath, looking up at Old Man God. He looks back, stops, stands a while, and then carefully puts her down in the grass.

"Have you come to your senses yet, child?" he asks. "Out of your wits with fright, eh? Now you'd better run home double quick, or you'll catch cold."

Then he turns round and walks off.

Josephine follows him with her eyes. She sees him going towards Angel Brook, across the little bridge into the dark wood, where he disappears.

She gives a sigh of relief.

Telling him about the cherries did the trick!

II

SOMETIMES you make me so angry," says
Mama, and her little yellow bun at her neck bounces
up and down.

Mama always gets angry with Josephine.

Mandy gets cross.

"Yes, I'm getting very cross with that girl," she
says.

And Agneta, who has just come home, gets irritated.

"That child makes me irritated," she complains.

Angry, cross, irritated—that's what they are, just
because Josephine has cut her hair. And her dress.
Now all the scissors in the house have to be hidden
away!

And she doesn't get any pudding and has to go

straight to bed after dinner, as a punishment. So she won't see Anton Godmarsson today. And not tomorrow, either! Because tomorrow she has to go to town all day. She's to have her hair cut properly and do errands with Agneta. Her own haircut simply won't do; it's got to be trimmed, Mama says.

Now they just talk *about* Josephine, but don't say a word *to* her, even though she's standing right there. And from their voices you'd think they were talking about the worst disaster that could possibly have happened. Josephine stands there with her back turned, staring obstinately out of the window. She doesn't say a word. But she thinks a great deal.

They are impolite to her, and nasty. But if they only knew what a close shave she's had—almost taken away by Old Man God! What would they say if they knew? Then they'd be sorry! Unfortunately she doesn't dare tell them about it, because then they'd find out she's been to Angel Brook. As things are, they think she got all wet from the hose in the churchyard, and that's just as well.

But really it doesn't matter a scrap what they think, because tomorrow will be fun anyway. Because then she's going to town . . .

The bus stops in the market-place in town. It's full of people moving about. Flags are flying everywhere. The sky is blue, and the flags are bright against it. Up there woolly white clouds are flying; it's windy, but in the streets the sunshine is lovely and warm.

A boy comes by, selling little paper flags. Agneta buys two.

"Do you know what they're for?" she asks.

No. Josephine doesn't.

"They're for us to wave to the King," says Agneta, giving Josephine one. "He's coming to town today."

Well, that was a surprise! So that's why so many people are out!

First Josephine has her hair cut. That doesn't take long, and afterwards she looks very much as she always did, except that her hair is shorter. Then they do their shopping. Today Agneta isn't the least bit irritated with Josephine, and all that nasty business of yesterday has been forgotten. That's the best thing about Agneta, about all of them at home. They get cross all of a sudden, but then forget all about it just as quickly.

Today Agneta is talking and laughing all the time.

They drink a glass of milk and eat a sandwich in the little restaurant in the park. Jackdaws and sparrows hop about on the grass, picking up crumbs that have fallen from the tables. Between the trees squirrels run about, so tame they almost eat out of Josephine's hand. They have a lovely time.

Agneta's curly hair blows in the sunshine. It is thick and lovely to look at. How beautiful Agneta is!

Josephine would like to tell her so, but such things are hard to say. Instead she suddenly puts out her hand across the table to pat Agneta's hair. As she does so she upsets the glass of milk, so that the milk splashes all over both of them. Agneta gives a cry. The sun goes under a cloud. And for a moment the whole day looks as though it's going to be spoiled.

But at that moment Eric is there, standing beside their table. And the sun comes out from behind the cloud again.

"Just a spot of milk," says Agneta, laughing. "It'll soon dry in the sun."

Eric has brought a balloon, a white one with a big blue parrot on it.

"This is for you," he says to Josephine, "so we don't lose you in the crowd around the King."

He fixes it to a button on Josephine's cardigan. Like a lovely cloud it floats about over her head. If only the village children could see her now!

The King is to make his speech in Castle Park. Everyone is going there with flowers and flags in their hands. Here and there a balloon waves. But no one has a balloon with a blue parrot on it, like Josephine's.

Down by the duck pond a red balloon flies away, and a little boy starts to yell loudly. Josephine gives an extra turn to the balloon string round her button.

More and more people gather. They jostle one another and laugh and talk. Then—a silence.

The King is coming!

But then a big brass band comes, too, and stands there blowing and tooting right in front of the King. Eric lifts Josephine up, and for a brief moment she sees the King's hat, but that's all. Then he must have taken off his hat, for afterwards Josephine sees no more. Eric puts her down. Everyone cheers and waves flags. The music plays. The King is going to speak, but a lot of other old men talk first.

After a while Josephine notices that Eric and Agneta are no longer standing beside her. She searches for them a while, but soon she gets tired. There are too many people here. She goes off towards the castle, her balloon waving above her head. No one else is walking about over here. She arrives at the big gates and walks into the courtyard. Not a soul in sight.

Now she can hear the King talking down in the park. But she still can't see him, even so. What fun it is being on her own here. And how exciting! No one lives in it any more. It's full of holes. Only one of its towers is undamaged: you could live in there. She looks around her.

Then she catches sight of two boys clambering about on the castle wall. They're terribly high up, and they wave to her.

"Want to come up?" one of them calls. "You can see better up here."

"She's just a kid! Can't you see she wouldn't dare?" say the others.

But she does. They'll see!

She runs up to the wall and begins climbing up the great stones that stick out of it. The nicer of the boys comes down and gives her a helping hand. After a shaky moment, there she stands, on the parapet.

Up there she finds a little path, rather narrow, with grass on it. It makes her feel a bit giddy, gives her a funny feeling in her stomach to look down from such a dizzy height. The boys rush back and forth, chasing each other on the wall. They're not frightened in the least.

But they had forgotten all about her, and the next moment they have vanished. There she stands! All alone on the high wall, and no way to get down. She thought the boys would help her.

Down in the park she can hear cheers. The King has stopped talking. The music plays again. People begin moving again. They go up to the castle, waving their flags. Josephine sits down on the castle wall and waits. What can she do?

If only she could see Eric and Agneta among all those people! Eric could help her!

But how is he to know she is sitting up here? How can she get him to look up?

Yes—now she knows!

Quick as a flash she takes off her shoes, loosens the balloon from the button on her cardigan, ties her shoes to the string, and runs along the parapet to the courtyard gate. At the very moment when the King's car sweeps into the courtyard, she lets go of the balloon. Slowly it floats down to the ground. And as the King gets out of his car, a pair of red shoes, dangling from a balloon, land right in front of him.

A man rushes forward to take the balloon away, but the King gets there first. Amazed, he picks it up and looks at the shoes. Several more official-looking men hastily gather round him.

Outside the castle now, the ground is black with people, and suddenly a murmur arises among them. They've caught sight of Josephine and are staring up at her in terror.

Now the King sees her, too. Josephine curtsies and waves her flag. After all, she hasn't been introduced to him before. The King waves to her, and the men all around him look jittery, and cross, too.

"Stand quite still, and we'll rescue you," shouts the King. He promptly sends one of the jittery gentlemen, who, puffing and panting, starts to clamber up the wall. He looks red in the face, and frightened, even though he uses a ladder, which someone has brought in haste from the castle.

Grabbing Josephine, he says through his teeth: "You little rascal!" Then, silent and furious, he climbs down again with her dangling under his arm.

It all happens in a flash. Suddenly she is standing in front of the King, who returns her shoes and the balloon.

"These must be yours, I think," he says, smiling.

"Yes," whispers Josephine.

"What's your name?" asks the King.

"Josephine."

"That's a pretty name. And your second name?"

"Joandersson."

"Josephine Joandersson," says the King. "You have a very lovely balloon. I think it's the prettiest I've seen."

Then Josephine unties her shoes from the balloon and hands it to the King.

"It's yours, Your Majesty," she says in a solemn voice. "Thank you for helping me."

But he doesn't want to take it from her.

"Oh, yes," she says.

He looks delighted, and thanks her for it; then he continues his tour of the ruins, carrying his balloon and with all the nervous gentlemen after him.

Josephine runs out through the courtyard gate. After a little while she comes across Eric and Agneta.

"What luck we've found you," says Agneta. "I was beginning to be worried. Where have you been all this time?"

Josephine replies evasively. But as Eric is driving them home in his car, he asks suddenly:

"What have you done with your balloon, Josephine?"

"I gave it to the King," replies Josephine.

"What a fib," laughs Agneta.

And that's the last that's said of the matter.

But when Mama opens her newspaper next day she gives a little cry of astonishment. Everyone gathers round her.

On the front page is a photo of the King. He is holding a big balloon with a parrot on it, and in front of him stands a little girl, suspiciously like Josephine.

Under the photo is written: "Josephine Joandersson presents a balloon to His Majesty."

Everyone finds the whole thing quite extraordinary. Mandy clasps her hands together, saying over and over:

"Well I never! Josephine, and the King himself!"

But Josephine doesn't think it's so very strange. One day she met Old Man God. The next day why shouldn't she meet the King?

12

"At Arontorp there blooms a rose,
Falalderol, falalderol
And I went my way, falalderol
From the roses that bloom on the shore—O"

JOSEPHINE has just awakened. Her window is wide open. The curtain stirs lightly, the sun is looking in, and the birds are twittering.

"A jack-tar am I, falalderol
Falalderol, falalderol
An ancient old jack-tar am I, am I
And the sea is my countree—O"

Listening in astonishment, she sits up in bed. Who can it be? She's never heard an old man singing in her garden before! Now he's whistling, too, the same lilting tune. She'll have to get up and have a look. But no sooner does she reach the window than she draws back, terrified, and hides behind the curtain.

It's Old Man God! Right under her very window, digging in the rose-bed! What is he doing here? Can't he stay up in heaven? Now he's singing again! "Falalderol!" What will Papa-Father say about this?

Josephine becomes quite indignant for Papa-Father's sake. Every Sunday he stands in the pulpit and says such nice things about Old Man God, and now what does Old Man God do? He sings sailors' songs in their garden! Is that the proper way to behave? At the very least, he could sing hymns! If people find out that this is how he carries on, they'll stop going to church. Now what's he singing?

> *"For many a year I've swallowed salt,*
> *Falalderol, falalderol*
> *For many a year I've swallowed salt,*
> *And that's why I'm so thirstee—O"*

Josephine has never heard such nonsense! Obviously, you get thirsty if you swallow salt. Maybe he has a sore throat? Sounds a bit hoarse, anyway. They usually make her gargle with salt when she has

[95]

a sore throat. It tastes horrible. But she doesn't go and *swallow* the salt.

Yes, Josephine is seriously disappointed with Old Man God. But scared, too. Why's he dawdling around down there, just under her window? Is he sorry he let her go? And what's he doing to the roses? Binding them up—but that's the gardener's job!

And then—suddenly—it dawns on her.

The new gardener! She hasn't met him yet. His name is Anton Godmarsson. The very first time she heard it, she thought there was something mysterious about his name, and said so to Mama.

And why was Granny Lyra so scared when she heard that Anton Godmarsson was coming to them? Of course—because she knew who he really was!

And now Josephine knows, too.

She thinks of all the things Papa-Father has said about Old Man God. How he made heaven and earth and was pleased with all he had made. Then he created the animals and people, to live on the earth and look after it. Then he had to come down at times, and keep an eye on his creation. And then he dresses up in disguise and shows himself only to certain people. Often he dresses up as a gardener . . .

A gardener!

And Anton Godmarsson was just the right name!

Yes, Josephine understands all right. But then why doesn't Papa-Father recognize him? He who has seen so many more pictures of Old Man God than Josephine has? *She* recognized him at once.

Maybe he doesn't *want* Papa-Father to recognize him. That's how he is, sometimes. He only lets *some people* know who he is—those he wants something from, no one else.

In other words, only Josephine! It's she he's after. What a frightful secret! But maybe it isn't Old Man God, after all. Maybe she's made a mistake? Oh, if only she has!

She remembers the book, given her by Papa-Father, with a picture of him in it. Now she slips over to the bookshelf and picks out the book, turning its pages. There's the picture! Silently she creeps over to the window again, comparing him with the book.

No doubt about it. It's the spitting image. The hair, beard, eyes, nose: everything. In reality he's a bit more wrinkled, but perhaps they've made the picture prettier, or else he has grown more wrinkled since they took it.

But that is he all right; there's no doubt about it.

Just then he catches sight of her: and for a moment they stare at each other. Then Josephine says seriously:

"So it's you, is it? You're here again?"

He replies:

"Why, if it isn't my little angel from Angel Brook. I was just wondering where she'd gone to."

Josephine doesn't reply; he goes on speaking to her:

"Mandy in the kitchen just said you were asking after me, and I've been looking around for you. But yesterday you were in town, visiting the King. I saw you in the newspaper."

"The King's all right," says Josephine, "he's nice

and kind." Looking him in the eye, she adds: "He doesn't turn little children into angels."

Then Old Man God laughs, but Josephine keeps staring at him.

"I'm naughty and sinful, and I'm not going to get any better," she says, emphasizing every word.

But he just pulls at his beard and winks at her.

"There's nothing naughty about you, little Josephine. It's all in your head."

Josephine is at a loss for words. He doesn't believe her! Now he puts his great hand over his eyes, looking up into the sky. Up there it's as blue as his shirt. A couple of tiny clouds are sailing overhead, as white and woolly as his hair and beard.

"We won't get rain today, either," he says. "And we needed it, too. But we won't get any yet."

Is that what you've decided? Josephine wonders.

"Man proposes but God disposes," he replies. And a shiver goes right through poor Josephine. Silent, wide-eyed, she just stares at him. He smiles. From the way he stands there you can see how sure of himself he is. He disposes, he says. He means he can dispose of Josephine, too.

Hastily she leaves the window, but at once runs over to it again.

"I'm going to eat from the forbidden tree again," she calls down, threateningly. "Every single cherry! You'll see!"

13

GRANNY LYRA is baking bread when Josephine comes to see her. Her kitchen is hot and smells of buns and biscuits, which are spread out everywhere on plates.

Granny Lyra herself flies about her kitchen like lightning, with flour all over her face. Normally pale, she looks ghostly in the dark, hot kitchen. But she is happy to see Josephine, and her eyes gleam like burning coals when Josephine gives her the flowers she picked on the way.

"Now you're really in luck, Miss, to come just when Granny Lyra's been baking," she says. "And I was in town yesterday, too. Granny Lyra always keeps her word. Yes, you'll see."

As usual, she goes on talking as she puts the flowers in water.

"How lovely they are; thank you, my pretty one. You're good-hearted, you are."

But "good" is a word Josephine has heard enough of. It fills her with fear.

"No," she says with emphasis. "I'm bad!"

The coal-bright eyes gleam with curiosity. "What's the matter? Have they been nasty to you again? Tell Granny Lyra all about it."

Josephine doesn't reply; she just takes one of the biscuits off the baking tin, to show how bad she is.

"Well, I understand," says Granny Lyra, "you don't want to tell on 'em—or even to think about it. In a moment I'll get you some lemonade and fresh-baked buns, and then we'll see what I've gone and bought in town. Something very special!"

Josephine brightens. She has an idea what it's going to be. But she'd be so much happier if all this business of the new gardener had never happened. It makes her feel gloomy and apprehensive, and she wanders to and fro in the kitchen, while Granny Lyra boils some coffee and serves up her buns.

"Well, it isn't easy to be little, no, it isn't," Granny Lyra sighs, shaking her head over Josephine, "poor little mite, it isn't easy for you, I know. But now we're going to have a little party. We'll have it in the bower, as usual, eh?"

Josephine thinks to herself that Granny Lyra is probably the only one who knows who Anton Godmarsson really is. She'd like to ask her but doesn't know how to begin. Then suddenly Granny Lyra says of her own accord:

"So you've got that Godmarsson up there at the vicarage, have you? What's he like, eh?"

Josephine asks breathlessly:

"He isn't a real gardener, is he?"

"No more than my old shoes," Granny Lyra replies. Taking out the last baking tin, she slams the oven door shut.

But Josephine feels she must have a straight answer.

"Who is he, then?" she asks.

Granny Lyra sucks at her tooth in an ominous way and says:

"*Can't you see that a mile off?* That's what I think, anyway. Never in all my life would I have thought he'd wangle himself into a vicarage!"

That's enough, and more than enough. Josephine doesn't need to know another thing. In a way it's a relief to have her suspicions confirmed. Clasping her hands, she says fiercely:

"He won't fool me, anyway!"

Then they go out into the garden, into the little bower, with the coffee, the lemonade, and all the

other good things. Last of all, Granny Lyra carries out a big parcel and lays it on the bench. But first they must eat.

As usual, Josephine eats her fill, and as she stuffs herself, Granny Lyra says as usual how sorry she is that they're starving her. But today Josephine doesn't find her own fate quite so tragic, her thoughts being entirely on what is in the parcel.

Several times she picks it up to open it, but each time she feels she wants to wait one minute more, have one more bun, one more biscuit . . . At last she can't swallow another bun or biscuit. She picks up the package, and sits a while with it on her knee.

The birds are twittering in the sky, bumble-bees are buzzing in the bower, and Granny Lyra is sucking her tooth. From inside the package, when she turns it over, comes a faint "ah-aaa". Josephine turns it over again: "ah-ah, aaa-aaaa!"

Then she opens it.

"It cost me thirty kroner and eighty orë," says Granny Lyra, just as the doll's head appears out of all the tissue paper.

Josephine gasps.

The doll can blink.

She has a hole in her mouth and can eat.

She can go to the lavatory.

And she can walk. As she puts out her right leg she looks to the right; as she puts out her left leg, she

looks to the left. She has fair, almost white, hair with
long ringlets, and her face is painted in bright colours.

"Isn't she lovely, eh?" asks Granny Lyra.

Yes, she's lovely. Josephine thanks Granny Lyra.
The doll takes a step and stares at her.

"I think her name ought to be Goldilocks,"
Granny Lyra suggests.

"Yes," whispers Josephine.

"Aaa-aaa," says Goldilocks.

Then Josephine gives her some lemonade. Immediately, Goldilocks wets her pants. But the biscuits stay put inside her. Josephine stuffs her with food.

Just then, brother Justus comes home. Granny Lyra gives him his dinner in the kitchen. Josephine is left all by herself for a while in the garden with Goldilocks.

She sits quite motionless in the grass, gazing at her. What a dress! Gauze with frills, laces, golden ribbons, and pink bows.

Goldilocks is the most perfect doll there ever was. She can do everything.

And Josephine is the most ungrateful little girl there ever was.

Because she doesn't like Goldilocks.

14

WHAT ON EARTH'S the matter with Josephine?"

"She isn't herself!"

"Surely she can't be ill?"

As soon as Josephine is mentioned, people start asking questions. Everyone is worried about her. But Mandy thinks she knows what the trouble is. She nods wisely and says:

"It's all that running to the harpy in the woods, of course. Goodness knows what ideas she's been putting into her head!"

"But Mandy . . ." says Mama.

And Mandy purses her lips and looks like someone who knows best. She insists on calling Granny Lyra "the harpy in the woods".

"What, running off to old harpy again?" she calls after Josephine.

Josephine doesn't get angry with Mandy, for since she got Goldilocks she knows—even though she can't explain it—that it's possible to dislike something that's quite perfect. In her way Granny Lyra is perfect, but Mandy doesn't like her. And that's all there is to it. Josephine understands Mandy. She even feels a sort of secret satisfaction at Mandy's outbursts. She assures Mandy that Granny Lyra is the kindest person in the world, but isn't offended when Mandy just snorts and contradicts her. Mandy has a perfect right to think whatever she wants to think.

Even so, Mandy hasn't got to the bottom of the

mystery. If she had, she wouldn't sit with Anton Godmarsson in the kitchen all day and let him call Josephine "the little angel".

This upsets Josephine more than anything else. There's no one to whom she can confide her terrible secret. No one realizes who Anton Godmarsson really is. Of course they don't; he doesn't *let* them. It's Josephine he's after, her and no one else.

So, it's useless talking to anyone. Josephine must fight him alone—now, as she did by the stream. Nothing seems to work. Four whole days have gone by, and she has tried everything. But there he still is.

She has stopped saying her prayers at night.

She doesn't join in saying grace at table.

She eats the fruit of the forbidden cherry tree.

Nothing does any good!

She has filled his hat with dandelion fluff.

She has planted thistles in his boots.

And he just laughs!

Josephine is absolutely exhausted. Nothing is so tiring as having to be naughty all the time. Even the forbidden cherries don't taste good any longer; they just make her feel sick.

No wonder she runs off to Granny Lyra whenever she can. At Granny's house, she's safe from Anton Godmarsson, for he never comes there.

And at Granny Lyra's biscuits and buns and

sweets are always waiting for her. And Goldilocks.
Josephine stuffs both herself and Goldilocks with tit-
bits. And yet—even here she doesn't feel happy.

Worst of all, she has been nasty to Goldilocks,
who is the most perfect doll there ever was. Still
worse—she isn't nice to Granny Lyra, either, who is
the most perfect granny there ever was.

Whatever has got into her?

It's hard to be nasty to Anton Godmarsson. But to
be nasty to Granny Lyra is as easy as falling over.
How strange everything is!

When she gets a bag of raspberry drops from
Granny Lyra, she just turns her nose up at them and
says she'd rather have licorice all-sorts. Then, with
an expression of disgust on her face, she swallows the
whole bag. That's the sort of girl she's turned into!

And Granny Lyra knits clothes for Goldilocks.
Josephine nags and orders her to knit more clothes
and still more; but when the clothes are ready, she
doesn't pay any attention to them. Yes, that's the sort
of girl she has become!

Granny Lyra continues to hold Josephine on her
knee just as she always did and feel sorry for her.
This puts Josephine into the worst possible humour.
She thinks up new things to complain about—things
which perhaps *might* be true, but aren't.

No, Josephine isn't herself.

The sun shines from morning to evening, day

after day. Every evening Anton Godmarsson looks up at the sky and says: "No rain tomorrow, either . . ." then tomorrow comes, and the sun shines.

The grass loses its greenness, the flowers wither . . .

15

THE NEXT DAY, when Josephine is on her way home from Granny Lyra, she discovers that she has left her monkey behind and turns back at once to fetch him. The monkey isn't in the bower or in the garden; he's lying on the veranda. And there sits Goldilocks, too, lolling backwards, her eyes half closed and her mouth open.

Josephine looks at her with a feeling of disgust.

Goldilocks has put on a terrible lot of weight. It's all the food Josephine has been stuffing into her. She seems able to hold any amount of it. Her mouth is always gaping for more. Of course, it isn't her fault, but it's not very nice. And just recently Goldilocks has begun to suffer from bad breath, too.

Josephine pokes her in the tummy, so that she jerks up straight and flutters her eyelids in a giddy way.

"Don't be so silly!" mutters Josephine. She takes her monkey and is about to go, but just then Granny Lyra's voice is heard from within the cottage. She hasn't seen Josephine. She's sitting at the telephone, talking.

This would have been of no interest to Josephine, if she hadn't heard Anton Godmarsson's name mentioned. She stops short as she hears:

"Of course. He's up there, digging and singing his silly songs. Drunk, too, I shouldn't wonder. Yes, Josephine's so scared of him she's almost jumping out of her skin. You'd think a clergyman might see what he's got in his house."

To listen to other people's telephone conversations is a nasty, sly thing. But Josephine just stands there, white as a sheet, her whole body paralysed. Granny Lyra goes on:

"Oh dear, yes, there'll have to be a change up there sooner or later. And it's a real shame about that little girl. They're so horrible to her. They beat her until she's black and blue and starve her too. Every time she comes here she's half-famished, and thin as a rake. And so badly dressed! She says her mother can't lift a needle, and that's why she never comes to the sewing circle. You know how it is with the table-cloth for the bazaar. Josephine doesn't think it'll be ready this autumn, either . . ."

Josephine goes red then white in the face, by

turns. Who in the world has betrayed such information? Who said the table-cloth wouldn't be ready? Surely Josephine can't have . . .?

"Yes, yes, we've got a funny lot up at the vicarage," Granny Lyra goes on. "The Vicar himself, he's so up in the blue, he hardly knows his own name."

How can she say such a thing about Papa-Father! How *can* she . . . Now she's talking about Josephine again:

"Yes, and the girl's got the wickedest temper, you wouldn't believe how bad-tempered she can be. But one can't blame the poor little thing, after all, she hasn't been properly brought up. They never give her a thought, they don't. She comes and sits on my knee and says Granny Lyra's all she's got in the world. Well, it's a disgrace . . . Oh, yes, what I'm telling you is true, Josephine told me everything herself."

Josephine can't listen to another word. There's a rushing noise inside her head, and she dashes away at such speed that Goldilocks rolls off her chair with a little "aa-aa".

Clutching her monkey tightly, she runs, without once looking back.

It suddenly strikes her that she ran away from Granny Lyra in exactly the same way once before—the time she ran off with the kittens, and thought she'd fallen into the clutches of a witch. That was before she got to know Granny Lyra. Now she

knows better—or does she? But surely she can't have chosen a witch for her granny? It was raining that time, a long while ago. Since then not a single drop has fallen. The sun is scorching and it's intolerably hot. Everything is dry and thirsty. Granny Lyra's words buzz inside Josephine's head.

Whoever said they beat her at home? Because they haven't, ever. Who said she never gets any food? Who said . . . surely, she can't have said it? Did she ever say that Granny Lyra is all she has in the world? Or has Granny Lyra been making things up?

What about Josephine? Hasn't she, too, been making things up? A feeling of indescribable terror grips her, a sudden insight: yes, she's the one who's been telling these stories! It's all her own fault. She told Granny Lyra quite a lot of things about them at home. She didn't really mean what she said; she thought Granny Lyra would forget everything, just as she had herself. And she thought Granny Lyra understood it wasn't all completely true, not word for word. Though it *could* have been, if . . . well, if they'd been nasty to her at home, though of course they weren't . . .

Yes, Josephine had made all this up herself. She'd done it when she'd been sulking, when she'd been in a huff with them at home. She'd done it so that Granny Lyra would be sorry for her and give her biscuits and sweets. That's the ugly truth. Granny Lyra always listened to her; it was as if she *wanted* to be sorry for Josephine. Sometimes it felt lovely, but sometimes Josephine didn't feel like telling stories. Even so, Granny Lyra always found a way to persuade her to talk.

Oh, what a muddle it all is! Everything goes round and round inside her head. Now the road to Granny Lyra's, which once seemed so attractive, seems terrifying. She shivers, even though the air is hot. The grass crackles lifelessly under her feet; the leaves are so dry they rustle at the least breath of wind. The ripe raspberries are also drying up; in the bushes a swarm of wasps is buzzing, and the flowers are all drooping. Nature is dying of thirst. Josephine hasn't thought about it before; but now she sees how parched everything is.

Then she remembers a walk she took with Papa-Father last spring. It had been raining; they looked at the raindrops and Papa-Father told her about them. He said the earth is the raindrops' heaven, and that we must make things as nice and beautiful for them here as we can.

Suddenly Josephine understands why there hasn't been any rain, and why Anton Godmarsson can look up into his heaven every evening and say: "No rain tomorrow, either!"

It's all her fault. She's made everything so nasty and ugly on earth that no raindrops want to come down! Poor little raindrops, poor little flowers.

Now she sees it all, but what can she do?

If she's good, Old Man God will take her away! That's why she has to be bad. But if she goes on being bad it'll never rain again!

What an awful muddle she's made of things! And all because she was disobedient and ate from the forbidden cherry tree and went to dangerous Angel Brook.

16

THAT NIGHT Josephine has a dream.

She dreams that she is a very tiny little animal, no bigger than a field mouse. Maybe she really is a field mouse, she can't be too sure. She has soft fur—like angels' down, says Papa-Father.

Someone is keeping her in an old shoe box, and she runs round inside it, quite contented with her existence. No harm can come to her here; she feels as safe as can be, until she hears an unknown voice complaining that she doesn't get any food. They're starving her, the voice says.

Are they? Josephine didn't know that; but now all of a sudden she realizes how hungry she is. She gets a pain in her tummy, and she is so weak she just has to lie there. Then someone comes—why, if it isn't Goldilocks!—with a bag of licorice all-sorts, and pours the whole lot into the shoe box. How big Goldilocks has become! How quickly she has grown.

The licorice all-sorts roll about in the cardboard box with a lovely smell. They are much bigger than the tiny creature Josephine has become. But that doesn't matter: she can swallow them almost whole anyway. One after another she swallows them, until they are all gone. Yet she still doesn't feel particularly full, just very thirsty. But it's no good thinking about water, she knows, because no rain ever falls on the earth any more.

Then she hears the unknown voice again. It is saying that no one can eat licorice all-sorts much bigger than oneself without bursting.

"Oh dearie me, she's going to burst," says the voice.

"Oh dear," says Goldilocks, who is standing leaning over the cardboard box, huge as a giant, looking down at Josephine from under her half-closed eyelids.

Almost out of her wits with terror, Josephine begins running round and round to digest the licorice all-sorts as quickly as possible. If only she could get out of the box, she would have more room to run about. Then maybe she could escape. She clambers and flops, while Goldilocks leans further and further over the box, gaping at her with her wide-open mouth and staring eyes.

At last she gets up.

But at the top she gets caught in a tangled grey net. The net sways and rocks. A big yellow spider, much bigger than Josephine, comes scuttling across it towards her. It has flour on its face, and its eyes gleam like hot coals. The spider's web trembles as the spider comes nearer, and in her terror Josephine

gets hopelessly tangled, wants to scream but can't . . .

Then she wakes up.

She is dripping with sweat and all tangled up in her sheet. The pale, golden moon is shining in the window. She stares at it. Has it, too, got flour all over its face? A moment ago she was sweating, now she's shivering . . .

Next day Josephine is ill. She has a high temperature and is delirious. Several days pass before her fever goes down. Mama stays with her almost all the time, changing her night-gown and laying cold compresses on her forehead, lifting Josephine's head from the pillow and giving her something to drink. That part is lovely.

When the fever goes down at last, she is very weak. She lies quietly in bed, with big round eyes.

"Feeling better today?" Mama asks, as she stands there with a glass of fresh orange juice and a banana. "Doctor says you'll soon be well again, if only you'll eat a little."

But that's just what's so hard. Mandy makes her favourite dish, fish-cakes, but she can't eat them. She makes lovely stuffed cabbage, which is Josephine's next favourite, but she can't swallow even a morsel.

The doctor gives her medicine to make her hungry, but it doesn't help at all. Then the doctor shakes his head and says he doesn't understand, because he can't find anything wrong with her now.

"Why don't you want to eat, my little friend?" he asks Josephine. She just shakes her head:

"I don't know."

On her bedside table is a heap of lovely presents. A beautiful picture book from Papa-Father. A drawing pad and crayons from Mama. A little teddy bear from Agneta. A big pink pig from Eric. And cut-out dolls with lots of clothes, from Mandy.

Josephine is even given a fine big pair of scissors to cut them out with. But she doesn't feel like playing. She sits glumly turning the pages of the picture book, or holding the pad and crayons on her knee, without drawing anything.

There is one more present on the bedside table. She hasn't opened it yet, but it is in her thoughts all the time. She doesn't know if she dare open it. It's from Anton Godmarsson.

"Don't you want to see what Anton has given you?" asks Mandy.

"Later," says Josephine.

"I think you ought to. Anton keeps asking and wondering how Josephine is."

"Has it been raining while I've been ill, Mandy?" Josephine asks.

"Oh dear, no, it's so dry and wretched. But that's

nothing for you to worry your head about. It'll be all right in the end."

Josephine sighs—Mandy just doesn't know about all that.

When Josephine is alone again, she lies as still as can be for a while. Then, making up her mind, she picks up the present from Anton Godmarsson. It is wrapped in a big brown envelope. With shaking hands she opens it.

A whole sheet of book-marks. Josephine stares at them, horrified. All the book-marks are angels, lots and lots of fat little angels, flying about or standing and sitting on woolly clouds!

When Papa-Father comes into her room after a while, he is met by a sight that is half comical, half sad. Josephine is asleep. She is holding a pair of scissors in her hand, and all around her lie lots of little angels without heads. She's snipped off all their heads, every one of them.

Curly little angels' heads lie all over the floor.

17

AFTER A WHILE Josephine wakes up and sees Papa-Father picking up all the little angels' heads.

She lies silent, watching him. Will he be cross with her now? He picks up every single head, then looks at her.

"So, you're awake, child," he says gently. "Did you sleep well?"

"No," says Josephine.

"Oh, why not?"

"I don't know."

Papa-Father pulls up a chair and sits down at her bedside. She moves over closer to him and takes hold of the arm of his chair, so that he won't go away. Then he lays his hand on top of hers.

"What's the matter, Josephine?" he asks. "Why weren't Anton Godmarsson's angels allowed to keep their heads?"

And he smiles, as only he can.

"I don't know," says Josephine.

"Oh yes, yes, I'm sure you know."

Obstinately Josephine stares at Papa-Father's clergyman's collar. He pats her hand, and she shifts her gaze over to the lamp above his head, then over to the flowers in the window, where the sun is shining. At last she looks back at Papa-Father, at the soft grey curls over his temples.

"Look at me, Josephine!" he says.

Then she looks straight into his big grey eyes.

"How much time have you got, Papa-Father?"

"As much as you like."

Josephine draws a little breath, and lets go of the arm of his chair.

"Wait a minute," she says and jumps out of bed, runs over to the bookcase to fetch a book, opens it, and slips back into bed again.

She has turned to a page with a picture of Old Man God.

"Do you see who it is?" she asks, showing Papa-Father the picture.

"Of course. It's God."

"Take a good long look at him! Don't you see who it is?"

"Why, God, of course."

Papa-Father obviously doesn't understand.

"Don't you see—it's Anton Godmarsson?"

Then Papa-Father smiles.

"Yes, you're quite right. It really looks like him."

"I saw it at once," says Josephine, nodding importantly. "You can hear it in his name, too. I thought there was something mysterious about his name the moment I heard it."

Colour has come back into Josephine's cheeks, and her eyes are lively.

"And he's no gardener, either," she goes on, emphasizing every word, "no more than Granny Lyra's old shoes. Do you know what has happened?"

Papa-Father gives her a serious look, shakes his head. She grips his hand and tells him:

"It's Old Man God who's come here. You know he likes to come down to earth and pretend he's a gardener or someone. And he hasn't let anyone know who he is. Not even you, Papa-Father. Only me, because he wants to turn me into an angel. And that's why he sent me the book-marks, to tempt me, but I don't want to be an angel. I want to stay here."

Papa-Father listens very quietly while Josephine goes on with her story. She tells him how she wanted to go and swim and eat from the forbidden cherry tree, to fool the brook, but how it caught her even so; and how Old Man God came and wanted to make her into an angel at once. But when he heard she'd been eating the forbidden cherries, Josephine went on to say, he let her go. Then he changed his mind and came back for her. And now he's hanging about, biding his time, waiting until she is good enough to turn into an angel. That's why she has to be naughty

[127]

all the time. And that's why no raindrops want to come down to earth.

"Dear Josephine," says Papa-Father, when she has finished, "you must have had a terrible time!"

Josephine gives a silent nod. He strokes her hair.

"Angel-fluff," he whispers. But Josephine gives a start.

"Don't say that!"

Papa-Father smiles and tells Josephine to listen very carefully. She promises. He begins by saying that Anton Godmarsson isn't Old Man God at all. Not at all!

"Wouldn't I know if he were?" he asks.

"Maybe he doesn't *want* you to recognize him," persists Josephine.

Then Papa-Father answers that it's by no means certain Old Man God looks like he does in his pictures. No one knows what he looks like. Not even Papa-Father.

"Then how can they make pictures of him?" Josephine wonders.

"Well, people want to imagine him somehow," says Papa-Father. "And since no one can help loving a wise old man, that's what they make him look like."

"Then Anton Godmarsson *isn't* God?" asks Josephine.

She thinks the whole matter over carefully . . . yes, she sees it must be as Papa-Father says, but

then why does Granny Lyra say Anton Godmarsson
isn't a proper gardener?

"He's been a sailor all his life," Papa-Father explains. "It's only in his old age that he's worked as a
gardener, but he's very good at it."

"And so that's why he sings sailors' songs!" Josephine laughs, relieved. "I did think it was a bit odd
that Old Man God . . . But Granny Lyra also said
that he was drunk."

Papa-Father looks sternly at her.

"A lot of silly gossip," says he. "You mustn't listen
to things like that."

Then Josephine gets bright red in the face.

"I . . . I didn't mean to," she says. "I was only
fetching my monkey, and she happened to be sitting
at the phone, and I heard it, and . . ."

She breaks off, looking tensely at Papa-Father.

"Are there really such things as witches?"

"Why do you ask that? Have you met one, little
Josephine?"

Then Josephine flies straight out of bed on to Papa-
Father's knee.

"I don't know," she whispers. "But if witches
really do exist, I'm sure I'll be one when I grow up."

"Just now you were afraid of becoming an angel,"
says Papa-Father, smiling. "What's the connection?"

Josephine's nose turns very red, so she rubs it hard
against Papa-Father's shoulder. Then she confesses

everything. All that happened at Granny Lyra's comes out, from beginning to end—all the nasty spiteful things she said about them at home, which she didn't really mean. It was just for the sake of the sweets and biscuits and because Granny Lyra understood the art of being sorry for children. And she tells about Goldilocks, who can do everything, and how she doesn't like her and is nasty to her. And she has been nasty to Granny Lyra, too, even though the old woman has given her such nice things.

"She isn't my granny at all," Josephine finishes, seriously. "My granny would never talk like that about us on the telephone. She'd . . ."

Josephine falls silent, pondering what a real granny would or wouldn't do.

Then Papa-Father says:

"And now you believe Granny Lyra's a witch, and that you'll be one when you grow up."

Josephine nods.

"I don't think it's as bad as all that," says Papa-Father quietly. "Some people just don't go together. They make each other nasty and bad . . ."

"But she was nice too," Josephine interrupts, with a guilty conscience. "She gave me such a lot of things."

"It's a sad thing, but giving each other presents doesn't prove that people suit one another. It's much more important to bring out what is kind and cheerful in each other. You've always made magic like that with me, Josephine, and we've never needed any presents, have we?"

Josephine nods and gives him the hardest hug she can.

"I suppose we just suit each other," she whispers.

Then she ponders for a moment and adds:

"But won't we ever have any presents, then?"

"Oh yes," Papa-Father laughs. "Of course we will, but no more than is reasonable. In the long run it's no fun getting everything you want."

"No," says Josephine, "it isn't."

Then her glance falls on the angels' heads, which are lying in a neat heap on the bedside table. And beside them lie the little bodies in another neat heap. She looks at them miserably. Papa-Father reads her thoughts.

"Shall I go and get some mending tape?" he asks. When he comes back, he helps Josephine repair the angels.

It's not so easy to find the right head for the right

body. Papa-Father finds it particularly difficult, but it doesn't matter; it just makes the angels funnier.

"Your angels look too silly," Josephine titters.

"So I see," says Papa-Father, looking helplessly at them. "I'm no hand with angels. I suppose they're just making fun of me."

Josephine sticks a bit of tape on to the back of one angel's head and surveys her handiwork.

"Well, you've got me, haven't you? I'll never make fun of you," she says seriously.

In the middle of the night Josephine is wakened by a soft noise.

It is very dark in her room, and when she looks towards the window no moon is looking in, no stars.

The sound is a familiar one, a sound she has been longing for. It's the rain. The rain has come at last. The drops patter against the window-pane like little notes of music.

Josephine runs to the window and looks out over the garden.

"Welcome," she whispers, and feels as light as a raindrop. All the heaviness in her heart these last few days has gone, vanished.

She gives a happy laugh and jumps back into bed. Then she drops off to sleep, while the rain goes on drumming against the windows. The raindrops are coming down to earth again. And God is back in heaven.

On earth everything is as it should be.